A FAITH FOR
THIS ONE WORLD?

by the same author

The Household of God
The Reunion of the Church
Sin and Salvation
A South India Diary

A Decisive Hour for the Christian Mission
(*part author*)

A Faith For This One World?

J. E. LESSLIE NEWBIGIN

General Secretary of the International Missionary Council, formerly Bishop in Madurai and Ramnad of the Church of South India

WIPF & STOCK · Eugene, Oregon

Wipf and Stock Publishers
199 W 8th Ave, Suite 3
Eugene, OR 97401

A Faith for this One World
By Newbigin, Lesslie
Copyright©1961 by Beetham, Margaret
ISBN 13: 978-1-61097-709-8
Publication date 10/15/2011
Previously published by SCM, 1961

CONTENTS

Preface	7
I The End of Christendom and the Rise of a World Civilization	9
1 The Revolt Against the West	9
2 The Acceptance of Western Science	13
3 A Single World History	26
II Where Shall We Look for a World Faith?	30
1 Professor Radhakrishnan's View	30
2 Professor Toynbee's View	41
3 Professor Hocking's View	46
4 A Unique Revelation?	53
III By What Authority? The Presuppositions of Christ's Revelation	56
1 The Biblical Doctrine of Creation	61
2 The Biblical Doctrine of Sin	68
3 The Biblical Doctrine of Election	77
IV By What Authority? The Content of Christ's Revelation	84
1 That Which Has Come	84
2 That Which Is To Come	92
3 The End of History	94
V The Pattern of the Christian Mission to the Nations	106
1 The Missionary Character of the Church	109
2 Older and Younger Churches	114
3 The Groundwork of Partnership	118
4 One Household	124
Index	127

For Helen

PREFACE

THE William Belden Noble Lectures, given at Harvard University in November 1958, are here reproduced substantially as delivered. At some points material which had to be omitted at the time of delivery owing to shortage of time has been included. I have not attempted to change the style, which remains that of a spoken address. Chapters III and IV are an expansion and development of material originally written for the Amsterdam Assembly of the World Council of Churches and included in the volume *The Church's Witness to God's Design*.

I should be happy if I could report that the two years since the date of their delivery had been spent in preparing these lectures for publication. I have to confess that they have been spent—apart from other preoccupations—in hesitating about whether they should be published. It would have been better if their large generalizations had been buttressed by far more detailed study and documentation. Two years ago I was still living in the happy delusion that a move from the care of an Indian diocese to the work of the International Missionary Council would bring more time for such work. I have now regretfully to conclude that it is not so. These lectures must go as they are or not at all.

But in one respect the delay in publication is fortunate. They will be published on the eve of the Third Assembly of the World Council of Churches, in New Delhi. This event will certainly focus Christian thought upon the issues with which these lectures deal. The very act of convening an Assembly of the World Council of Churches in the capital city of India will raise in the sharpest form the question of the place of the Christian faith in the world of the non-Christian religions. The theme of the Assembly—*Christ, the Light of the World*—will challenge both Christians and non-Christians to consider the claim of Jesus to be the unique saviour of men. And the integration of the International Missionary Council and the World Council of Churches which is expected to take place at the New Delhi Assembly is in itself a challenge to all Christians to recognize the intrinsically missionary character of their churchmanship, and to reflect afresh upon the way in which this is to be expressed in the changed conditions of the twentieth century.

It remains only for me to express my gratitude to those who invited me to give these lectures, and who gave me unstinted hospitality and encouragement at the time of their delivery —especially President and Mrs Pusey, and Dr and Mrs George Buttrick of Harvard University. I shall always remember with thankfulness the days I spent in their company, as well as the stimulus of comment and question from those who attended the lectures. I must also thank Mrs Barss who was good enough to type out the material from a tape recording, and thus to remove my most immediate excuse for not publishing it, and Miss Gladys Mather who kindly compiled the index and helped with proof reading.

The founder of the Noble Lectureship placed on record the hope that, through these lectures, there might be aroused 'in young men, and primarily in the students of Harvard University, the joy of service for Christ and for humanity especially in the ministry of the Christian Church'. If these lectures do anything towards the fulfilment of that hope I shall be thankful.

LESSLIE NEWBIGIN
Bishop

I

THE END OF CHRISTENDOM AND THE RISE OF A WORLD CIVILIZATION

1. *The Revolt Against the West*

THE purpose of these lectures is to consider the claim of Christianity to be the faith for our world, in the situation of today. I shall be speaking from the background of my own experience as a missionary in India during the last twenty-two years. From that standpoint, the question 'Is Christianity a faith for our world?' is one that does not easily suggest an affirmative answer. For many thoughtful Indians today, it seems obvious that Christian missions belong to a chapter of world history that is closing. And I suppose that judgment would also be accepted by many in other parts of Asia and the Islamic world. For the rise of the modern missionary movement coincided with the cultural and political and economic expansion of the white races of Western Europe and North America, an expansion which has reached now every part of the globe. That expansion, having carried the influences of the white races into almost every part of the world, has now been halted and reversed. It is now no longer taken for granted that the leadership of the world lies in the hands of the white races. The political aspect of this reversal is familiar to us, dramatized as it is by the Bandung Conference and its aftermath. But perhaps one needs to spend some time in a country like India to feel the strength of the cultural and religious tide that now flows against the West. Among the peoples of Asia, representing something like one half of the world's population, there is a deep conviction that the most important fact of the modern world is not, as the Western nations think, the struggle between Communism and its alternative, but the ending of the global domination of the Western races and the development of the former subject peoples to their full cultural and political stature; that the great new fact of our time is the end of colonialism. This fact in itself profoundly alters the situation of the missionary movement which developed along with, and in some senses as a part of, the expansion, political, cultural and economic, of the white races. It means that Christian missions have now to work not with the tide but against it.

But when we look at the religious aspect of this reversal of the world's tide, the point becomes even clearer. Here let me speak specifically of India. Most of the early missionaries to India, of the modern period, took it for granted that in going from Christendom to Hindustan, they were going from a higher civilization to a lower, that they were taking light into darkness. They did not generally make a clear distinction between the gospel and the culture of Christendom. They even thought of the gospel as the crown of that culture. There was a famous debate in the General Assembly of the Church of Scotland in 1796 at which a motion to take a collection in aid of foreign missions was defeated. It is interesting to examine the arguments that were used to defeat that motion. The opponents of the motion argued that to try to teach Christianity to the untutored heathen was as absurd as to try to teach Newton's *Principia* to a man who did not know his ABC. Even those who supported the motion, those who sponsored foreign missions, were not free from the same confusion of the gospel with Christian culture. They were confident, overconfident as we see today, that an English education would be the most powerful way of bringing men to Christ. The foundations of the great work of Christian higher education in India were laid by the Scottish missionary, Alexander Duff. When he was once asked what he was doing teaching classes in English and philosophy and science when he ought to have been preaching the gospel, he replied that

The End of Christendom

he was laying a mine which in due course would explode and blow up the whole of Hinduism. On the evidence so far, one would be tempted to say that if Hinduism were a monolithic block, then the detonation of Duff's mine would certainly have shattered it, but that Hinduism is in fact not a granite block but a sandbank. The mine has gone off, but the sandbank has not disappeared; it has only changed its shape. That may, however, be too hasty a judgment, as we shall see later.

The earliest reaction of Indian culture to the invasion of the West was mainly passive. There were, of course, those who resisted it as the conservatives will always resist the unknown. But there were also multitudes who welcomed it, who in effect accepted Western civilization at its own valuation and tried to get a Western education for themselves and their children. The local culture did not have the inherent strength to master the incoming culture, to meet it on its own ground, to take what was assimilable and reject the rest while retaining its own identity. But today what is happening in India, and over most of Asia, and in the Islamic world, is a vast renaissance of these ancient cultures and religions, a renaissance stimulated precisely by the invasion of the Western culture, but having now in large measure succeeded in mastering that culture, and making it contributory to its own. Western culture is now made tributary to the ancient culture of India instead of being allowed to displace it.

It is always dangerous to indulge in large generalizations, but it would not be untrue to say today that Hinduism faces the world with a serene confidence in its own adequacy to the problems of human existence on this planet, with a conviction that it is indeed the religion for mankind. Those whose thinking is expressed in such writings as those of Radhakrishnan are sure that they have in the Hindu religious and philosophical tradition the whole full-orbed truth of which, for instance, Christianity and Islam are but partial and one-sided expressions. They are sure that in principle all truth is contained at least in germ in the ancient scriptures of India. They feel therefore free spiritually to plunge headlong into the stream of modern scientific thinking and technical development without feeling that thereby they are going outside the ocean of truth which is Hinduism. They can say in a certain sense 'all things are ours', whether ancient or modern, whether Western or Eastern. For in the Hindu position they feel that they have something at the same time infinitely stable and infinitely flexible. Moreover, they are sure that in the realm of practical politics also, Asia rather than Europe or America can offer the secret of peaceful co-existence among the nations of the world. They are sublimely sure that the recent period, in which the Christian West more or less explicitly asserted, and the rest of the world more or less tacitly admitted, the right to control the affairs of the nations is a closed chapter in world history.

Moreover, it is not simply that there has been a tremendous renaissance of the ancient religious cultures of the non-European races. It is also a fact of fundamental importance that the white races have so largely discredited themselves in the eyes of the rest of the world. In the early days of, for instance, the nationalist movement in India, there was a profound respect for the morals and culture of the West. That respect has been largely destroyed. Foremost among the reasons for this are the frightful wars which the white races have unleashed upon the world in the course of this century and which have shaken the whole world with their resulting convulsions. Second, there has been a discrediting of the ethical pretensions of the so-called Christian West. This has come about through the growing variety of contacts between East and West, the experience of Asians living and studying in the West, the distribution of literature, and the influence of the cinema. In India the ubiquitous cinema has been the means of introducing almost all strata of the population in the most vivid possible way to conceptions of ethics so much lower than their own as to make nonsense of any claim by the West to moral leadership. It would not be a too gross exaggeration to say that for many in the East the West stands for three things: war, sex and technics.

The third commodity has an infinitely expanding market; the rest of the world certainly wants our technics. It does not want our wars, and in its more responsible section, it does not want our morals. It is no longer possible to suggest in any educated audience in the non-white parts of the world that the civilization of the white man represents a higher level of morals and culture than that of the rest of the world.

2. *The Acceptance of Western Science*

Here, however, we come to an immensely important fact which must arrest our attention for some time: the rest of the world certainly recognizes the superiority of Western technics and is determined to have as much as possible of it as quickly as it can be got. In every part of the world, the desire to achieve higher standards of technical development, to master the means of exploiting natural resources and the methods of research which lead on to further technical achievement, has become one of the main driving forces of national life. It is not simply that it is through these means that the standard of living can be raised, though that is a very important factor. A country faced with the gigantic problems of India or China has no alternative but to try to exploit to the limit every possible means of increasing productivity. But it is also that this scientific technical culture which has developed in the West is now regarded as the world civilization of our time. It is regarded as something which is not specifically Western but universal, something in the sharing of which one shares in the civilization of mankind. The current demand for a fuller share in this scientific culture of our time is capable of producing some amusing eddies and cross currents in the general tide of anti-colonialism. In 1957 the Liberian delegate to the United Nations complained that his country suffered as compared with Ghana in not having had the advantage of being a colony. In India, the declared intention of the constitution that Hindi should replace English as the national language at the end of fifteen years appears likely to be unfulfilled, so great is the demand to retain English as a necessary window into the cultural and scientific world of which English is an important vehicle. This, it is often repeated, is not to go back to the struggles of the past decade. It is not to submit again to Western dominance. All that is emphatically rejected. It is simply to insure that one remains in the stream of world civilization.

What has happened then is that while the cultural and political and economic advance of the Western world has been halted, while the West's claim to world leadership has been repudiated, something has come into being which is recognized as a world civilization, something which, while it is indubitably a product of the West, is regarded as a detachable and potentially independent product, something potentially the property of all men equally. This view of the situation is shared by educated people both in the East and in the West. In India certainly, and probably in the rest of Asia, there is a strong conviction that one can take Western science and technology in the biggest available doses without the risk of damaging one's Eastern digestion. The large and able body of graduates from the science faculties of Asian universities, the students flocking to Britain, America and Germany for technical courses, the growing multitude of educated men and women going into industrial and mercantile enterprises of the Western type, these men and women are sure that they are not in any way cutting themselves off from their own religion and culture. They are sure that this world of technology, while it has originated in the West, belongs to the whole world, and that the East can take it on its own terms and use it in its own way. And in the West also we find thoughtful men holding the view that this new world civilization with its science and its technics, though formed in the matrix of Western Christendom is yet now a wholly independent entity which may be expected to live and develop without any necessary connection with the Christian civilization which gave it birth.

Moreover, there is at least a fairly strong case for the view

The End of Christendom

that the mother died in childbirth. The same century which has witnessed the global spread of this new technical civilization has witnessed also developments which many observers have characterized as the end of Christendom. The period in which Christianity was the folk religion of the peoples of Western Europe is at an end. The Christian faith is either explicitly repudiated or passively ignored by the majority of the people of the countries traditionally Christian. While innumerable features of the landscape remain to testify to the faith in which they were formed, they are now rather symbols of a past faith than expressions of a present one. Within its own territory, Christianity has largely failed to come to terms with the scientific and technological culture which it has brought to the birth. Even in its own home, the child pursues its course of development with apparent indifference to the existence of its parent. Moreover it is clear that for many in the so-called Christian West science has become more than merely an organized body of knowledge or a basis for technical progress. It has become itself a kind of religion. Multitudes of people look to the sciences as the ultimate source of truth. They see in science a body of finally reliable thought as contrasted with the myths and superstitions of religion. And if they have any hope of salvation from the ills that flesh is heir to, it is rather based on the achievements of science than on the promises of religion. This is one of the really decisive facts for our understanding of the modern world, that at the moment when our Western culture has penetrated the life of almost the whole of mankind, it has itself disintegrated; and that this disintegrated culture is itself disintegrating the ancient non-Christian cultures with which it is in contact. Western man has, on the whole, lost belief in the validity and finality of the revelation around which his culture originally grew up. Certainly this is not the whole truth. The remarkable revival in the life of the churches in the United States in the past decade is one of the facts to which attention would have to be paid in any fair survey, though the question how this revival is to be interpreted is one on which there would be differences of judgment. But at least it is beyond dispute that the Christian faith no longer provides the controlling principles of the culture of the white races of Western Europe and its offshoots. It is also beyond question that the science and technology which Western Christendom brought to the birth, and which are still primarily based in the Western world, have now become in an effective sense the property of all nations. What now effectively circles the globe is not the gospel which was to be preached to all nations, but rather that whole system of thought and practice which is loosely called 'scientific' and which is acting everywhere as a revolutionary power in the lives of peoples.

So impressive are these facts that it seems natural to take them as the basis for our thinking about the future of the human race. We have, it would appear, something like a world civilization in existence and showing every sign of vigorous growth. It is by many taken for granted that short of the catastrophe of an annihilating war, mankind as a whole will continue to move increasingly in the single universe of discourse provided by modern science, and to use the knowledge it provides to gain a greater and greater mastery over his world. The question therefore arises: 'What is the relation of Christianity, claiming to be a world faith, to this new world civilization? Can it provide a faith for this world? What is its relation in this task to other faiths? And what kind of purgation does it require to meet this new and universal task?'

Let us begin by asking: 'What exactly is this thing which has become a world civilization? What is its relation to Christianity?' It is agreed that it has been produced within the matrix of the old Christendom. But is it now totally independent of its origin? Is it a completely detachable part? Can it develop within the ancient non-Christian cultures without completely disrupting them? At first sight one would be inclined to answer the question in the affirmative. There is nothing specifically Christian about a mathematical theorem or a law in physics. Hindus and Buddhists are not a whit less able than Christians to be first-class scientists. In fact it seems that in some ways the ancient Eastern religions have less difficulty in absorbing modern scientific ideas than Christianity has had. There has been no struggle between science and religion in India or Japan comparable to that which took place in England in the nineteenth century. The predominantly monistic structure of Hindu and Buddhist thought is indeed more hospitable to the modern scientific world view than is the thought world of the Bible with its ineradicably dualistic notes. That is one of the reasons for the attractiveness of Eastern religion to modern Western man.

But reflection prompts further questions. Does the origin of this scientific world civilization within the old Christendom carry with it no lasting effects? Is it possible, for instance, that that restless curiosity about the natural world, that loving and precise interest in the minutest facts about the world of visible and tangible things, which has been a large part of the driving force of scientific discovery, can permanently co-exist with the belief that the visible world is an illusion? But that belief lies at the very heart of the view of life which finds expression in most Asian religion. This is not something accidental but goes to the heart of the difference between religions. Christianity can retain the faith in the reality and goodness of this visible world, can believe that it is the work of God's fingers and the object of his love and therefore a worthy object of our love, because Christ rose from the dead. Without that faith, the most obvious option open to us, and one obviously attractive to those in the West who have lost the resurrection faith, is the way of the Vedanta, the way which finds ultimate reality in the spiritual and sees the visible world as a veil of illusion which the wise man learns to strip off. If it should ever happen that any of you should visit the English Cambridge, you will find there an Institute of Polar Research at which there are preserved the sketches made by Edward Wilson during Scott's last expedition to the South Pole. I shall be surprised if you do not find yourself as deeply moved as I was to see them, to see how a man living at the very extremities of life, in circumstances when even to remain living was an almost superhuman achievement of courage, could devote himself to making minute and precise sketches of scenery, of birds, of animals, with the most careful notes as to the colours which should later be painted in when one reached a climate where paint would not freeze. I find it hard to believe that that kind of loving, tender interest in every bit of God's creation can permanently co-exist with the belief that the material world is an illusion.

But there is a far more fundamental point to be considered. The scientific world civilization whose nature we are considering is not simply a matter of abstract thought. Without spending time here on the origin and development of modern science, it is sufficient to say that what we are dealing with is in fact a whole complex. It includes firstly the body of knowledge and opinion which is usually called science; secondly the methods of purposive research by which this body of knowledge is always being enlarged; thirdly the multiplication of techniques and appliances of every description by means of which this knowledge is brought to bear on human life; and fourthly, as the driving power of it all, the widespread conviction that human life can be and ought to be changed. My point now is that without this last element, the modern development and world-wide spread of scientific ideas and methods would be impossible. Whatever may have been the case at the beginning of the modern scientific era, it is indisputable that the universal dissemination of the methods of thought and action characteristic of modern Western science is indissolubly related to the belief that by its means human life can be made better, fuller, healthier, richer than it has been in the past, and that human history ought to be understood in terms of the effort to make it so. This belief has become so familiar to us in the West that we generally forget that it runs counter to some of the deepest elements in the religious faith of at least half the human race. Most of the ancient religions of mankind have interpreted the movement of events in terms of recurrent cycles. The idea of linear movement in a single direction is incompatible with their deepest convictions. And indeed there is every reason in human experience for this. The dominant patterns of our own experience are cyclical, not linear. The cycles of days and weeks and years, of vegetable and animal life, of human birth, growth, old age and death, all naturally suggest an interpretation of history in cyclical terms. Indeed human institutions and civilizations apparently go through the same cycle of birth, growth, decay and death. Why, then, should it be suggested that any other pattern is determinative of history as a whole?

This cyclical interpretation of the events of history is the most natural one if, with the ancient Eastern faiths, one holds that Reality is essentially timeless and changeless spirit. Reality is, on this view, the centre of the spinning wheel, changeless and motionless. The movement of events does not alter that centre. What was there at the beginning is there at the end. The appearance of change is illusion. But—as will be obvious—if you introduce into this pattern of thought the idea of a non-cyclical change, that is to say the idea of irreversible linear movement, you have completely disrupted the pattern. A wholly different view of the nature of reality is involved.

In the part of the world where I have been living, in the Tamil country, years are counted by means of a sixty year cycle. Each one of the sixty years has its name, and at the end of sixty years, one returns to the beginning of the list. Thus, for instance, the year 1800, the year 1860, and the year 1920 have the same name, and apart from other evidence there is no means of distinguishing these years from one another. But India is now embarked upon a series of five year plans. There may possibly be twelve of them. It is not, however, anticipated that at the end of that period India will return to the point at which she was when the first five year plan was begun. The old cyclical pattern has been disrupted, and a new way of thinking has replaced it. It is therefore natural that it has become impossible to continue to use the old calendar, that it becomes necessary to use a linear calendar, and that in fact it is almost universal that the calendar which has the letters AD upon it is used.

It is one aspect of the spread of this one world-wide civilization that more and more people are coming to adopt that time reckoning which moves in a single irreversible line from the date of the birth of Christ. Is this merely an accident of history or is it a true symbol of the fact that in being brought into the sphere of modern world civilization nations are being related willy nilly to the fact of Christ? I shall show in a moment that that relation may be either positive or negative; that is not the point at the moment. The point is a two-fold one: first that this modern, scientific world civilization, whether in its communist or non-communist form, contains as an essential ingredient the idea and the fact of purposive change, an idea fundamentally incompatible with the cyclical time scheme of the ancient Eastern religions; and secondly, that this linear conception of time, and the place consequently given to purposive change in the whole view of life characteristic of the scientific world civilization, have found their way into Western civilization from the Bible. The view of the time process characteristic of the pre-Christian thought of Greece and Rome was cyclical, not linear. Zoroastrianism seems to have had its own understanding of human history in terms of a struggle between light and darkness leading to the victory of light. But it is unquestionably from the Bible, and more specifically from the Christian view of the meaning of human history, that these ideas have become the common property of Western culture. The belief in a new age to come is in fact a secularized version of the Christian belief in the coming of the Kingdom of God. The fact that more and more of the peoples of the world are brought to reckon the events of their lives on a time-scale which takes the coming of Jesus as the starting-point is not a meaningless trifle. It is a valid symbol of the fact that, in coming into the orbit of modern, secularized, Western civilization, they are being related *in some sense* to the fact of Christ. In what sense, we shall consider in a moment.

We are examining the view that the scientific world civilization of our time is an independent and self-sufficient entity which, though cradled within Christendom, is now quite independent of any particular religious faith. We have looked at two preliminary arguments against this view, namely that in respect of its valuation of the visible world, and in respect of its understanding of the time process, the scientific world view appears to be dependent on the Christian tradition. We must now scrutinize more carefully the whole idea of a secular, religiously neutral order of being. This idea is itself a product of the New Testament. It could not have arisen, for instance, within the world of Indian religious thought. In that world, visible and tangible things are understood as the veil which covers the inner reality, the veil which the enlightened learn to see through. They are all equally within the sphere of illusion. The workman who smears the sign of his god on the latest giant machine imported from America or Russia, and the managing director who resigns in mid-career to become a *sannyasi*, are equally in their different ways expressing their view of the relation of religion to this world. The idea of a secular order, of an order of reality, of a system of thought and practice which lies, so to say, outside of the direct responsibility of religion, but in which the will of God is to be done, is a Christian idea. As the word itself reminds us, it is rooted in the biblical concept of the two ages, the two *saecula*, this age that now is, and that which is to come which has already broken into this age in the coming of the Messiah. This in turn rests upon the biblical doctrine of creation which sees the sensible world as an order of being which is real, and yet has a provisional independence over against the God who created it. And finally it rests upon the doctrine of the fall, which means, as far as this present context is concerned, that this created order has become charged with forces which actively oppose the will of the Creator, and that the Creator even permits these forces to have a limited and provisional authority, an authority which cannot, however, overturn the final authority of the Creator himself. These familiar biblical doctrines provide the underlying substructure for the whole idea of the secular, and without them it could not have appeared. But the immediate basis of it is to be found in the New Testament proclamation that a new *saeculum*, a new age, a new world has dawned in Jesus Christ. In the light of this new dawn the present age is seen to be what it is, a world which has fallen under evil powers and which is therefore under judgment but which, nevertheless, God sustains in being in order to provide the scene within which the powers of the new age may work.

The relation between Christianity and the secular order is thus a dialectical one. Christianity has to confront the world of secular thought and life, in science, in politics, in technology, with its witness to the reality and power and claim of the new age; but it must not try to rob the secular order of its provisional autonomy. This autonomy, and therefore this duality, must remain until the Creator of all things in his own appointed time brings the old order an an end and consummates all things in the new order in Christ. From the point of view of the biblical faith, therefore, the world-wide spread of the secular world-view which Christianity has brought to the birth is not a religiously neutral event. It is not, for instance, simply part of the scenery for the Church's missionary enterprise. It is part of the working out in human history of the results of the coming of Christ. It is part of the process by which the coming of the Light of the world places all men in a critical situation, a situation charged with the possibilities both of ultimate salvation and of ultimate loss.

In the New Testament we see the breaking into this world of the new reality of the Kingdom of God present in Jesus. In the Johannine writings this presence is interpreted in terms of light breaking into darkness, and, because it is light, having the power of judgment. Every person upon whom the light falls is placed in a critical situation. The light exposes that evil which had hitherto been regarded as merely part of this world. Wherever the light falls, therefore, there are two alternative possibilities, and only two: either to shut out the light and reaffirm one's solidarity with this world order, or to come to the light confessing and thereby breaking one's solidarity with the world that lies in darkness. When this choice has been made, when Christ has really been encountered, history is placed on a new time scale. It is placed on a scale which runs from the breaking in of the new era to its full consummation, from Christ's coming to his coming again. It is a time scale which looks both back and forward, and in which a merely cyclical conception of human life becomes impossible. One sees in the gospel story how men are brought into the presence of the light and gently but inexorably led to the point where they must accept or reject it, must either give themselves wholly into the authority of the ruler of this age or enter the new age which begins in Jesus Christ. One sees the apostles going forth from Jerusalem and Antioch, continuing the same process with the declared intention that the gospel which brings both judgment and mercy shall be proclaimed to the whole earth so that all men and nations may be brought within its orbit. The coming of him who is the Alpha and the Omega, the beginning and the end of all things, precipitates a process of polarization, beginning with those who come immediately within his influence in the days of his flesh, and continuing to the ultimate limits of human history.

This understanding of the times in which we live is set before us in such apocalyptic sections of the New Testament as Mark 13 and the parallel passages. We misinterpret these passages if we forget that they are a prophetic interpretation of the days in which we live, the days between the coming of the Word made flesh and his coming again. They describe these days precisely in terms of a polarization of human history, culminating in the ultimate conflict between Christ and antichrist. The first characteristic of them is the appearing of false christs. The coming of the true Saviour precipitates the appearing of false claims to provide salvation for mankind. Life can no longer go round in circles. The question of man's ultimate destiny has been raised. Therefore human affairs become increasingly charged with messianic expectations. It is no longer possible to think of human life in terms of the wheel which always returns to its starting point. One must think in terms of total welfare—freedom from all the ills of human existence. Men expect messiahs, and get them. And history is the increasingly sharp drawing of the contrast between the true Omega and the various mirages that draw men to their doom with false hopes, between the true offer of total welfare on God's terms and the false offers of total welfare on other terms, between Christ and antichrist.

It is within this New Testament picture of the bringing of all the nations into the sphere of the one decisive act of judgment and mercy in Christ that we are to understand most inclusively the events of our time. It is becoming impossible for any nation on earth to continue to live within the cyclical time scheme of the ancient Eastern faiths or within the time scheme of any tribal or national history. What we are witnessing is the process by which all peoples are being drawn into a unitary world history. It is not merely that we have one science and one technology; it is that we have increasingly one world history in which we are all inexorably involved one with another. And the driving force of this one world history is the idea of a new order in the future. It is this secular messianism which gives to the world-culture of our time its power to disrupt great and ancient cultures and to draw their peoples into a single current—or rather cataract—of development. The 'new order' may be conceived in terms of the victory of the proletariat, of the triumph of technological development, of national liberation, or of the power and success of the great leader. These variants are all within the same essential pattern: a faith that there is a new order just over the horizon. 'The coming world civilization' is propelled by this secularized

The End of Christendom

form of the biblical faith in the coming of the Kingdom of God.

The peoples of Asia and Africa and the Islamic world, nurtured in non-Christian cultures, are all having to wrestle with issues which have been posed for them from within the Christian tradition. If one considers for a moment some of the problems which they are facing, this will be clear. The problem, for instance, of creating a welfare state is one which all the young nations have to tackle. It is totally impossible for them, having recovered national independence, to revert to the forms of government characteristic of the period before they fell under European dominance, and begin to rule after the manner of Hyder Ali or Tippu Sultan. Their common people have developed expectations which did not exist two centuries ago, expectations which owe their origin to the West and ultimately to the Christian tradition. Or consider the issue of human rights. Great difficulty was experienced by the constitutional lawyers of Japan when the new order was introduced because there was no suitable word in Japanese to express the idea of human rights. It had come as part of the Western tradition, deriving its main power from that valuation of the individual which the West learned from the Christian Gospel. Today it is an idea which has become one of the political realities with which every government has to reckon. Or consider the most pressing of all the problems with which the younger nations are wrestling, the population problem. Why has the equilibrium of world population been so violently upset? Because means for saving life, including both medical techniques and also means of transport and communication, means developed in the West, together with a valuation of the individual—even the apparently useless individual—which is a product of the Christian tradition, have so lowered the death-rate throughout the world as to create a huge imbalance between death-rate and birth-rate. None of these issues arises from within the ancient non-Christian cultures; all of them arise from the impact upon these ancient cultures of a culture derived from the Western Christian tradition, a culture which has as its central driving force a secularized form of the Christian eschatology.

3. A Single World History

Now this drawing together of all people into a common history is a radically new event. The world has not had, in this sense, a common history before. There have always been people who had, in the proper sense, no history, people, that is to say, who are living in a static situation, in which nothing is recorded because it is not believed that anything really happens. One can go, even now, into villages in India where that is true, where there are no records except those of the purchase and sale of land, and where no one could tell you the age of any building which was put up earlier than the age of the oldest inhabitant. I have always remembered the impression made upon me as a student by the first chapter of J. L. Myres' book *The Dawn of History*. It is entitled, 'Peoples Which Have No History'. It was a reminder that the greater part of the human race has indeed, in that sense, had no history. Today, these peoples who have no history are being drawn irreversibly into the current of a single world history.

And there are people who have had what one may call a tribal history, a conception of history in terms of their own people, a history which had its meaning in the struggles and achievements of a people over against the peoples round about him. Such history is summarized by '1066 and all that', or reckoned *ab urbe condita*. Perhaps those who have written history in these terms have really believed that these dates were the crucial dates in human history, but it is less and less possible for any single nation to regard its own history as the clue to world history. The affairs of this one world civilization press more and more upon all peoples, drawing them into the stream of a single unitary history. And this means that a situation of a quite new kind has been created for the human race. Tribal history is possible because the people of the tribe have some kind of belief concerning the origin and destiny of the tribe. The greatness of the tribe, its success against its enemies, its influence over surrounding peoples provide the criteria for determining which events are of historic significance. A world history is only possible if there is some kind of belief concerning the origin and destiny of mankind as a whole. There can be no common criteria for judging events, no basis on which some events are regarded as memorable and some not, unless there is some kind of faith regarding the meaning of human history as a whole, its beginning and its end. The very existence of a common world civilization, therefore, poses the question of the meaning of human life itself, in other words the question of religion. It is for this reason that a world culture cannot in the nature of the case remain religiously neutral. In so far as it is genuinely universal, it must necessarily raise the question of the ultimate destiny of man.

We have seen that the present technological world culture is the offspring of Western Christendom and that it derives its power from a secularized version of the Christian eschatology. But that statement has now to be developed further. The belief in progress which developed in Europe in the latter part of the eighteenth and the beginning of the nineteenth century, which substituted for the biblical vision of the kingdom of God the vision of a perfect human society to be enjoyed by future generations on earth, has been in the West largely destroyed by its own inner logic. The reason for this will be considered in a later lecture. The fact is that it has proved to be like one of those radioactive substances whose radioactive power is in direct proportion to the speed of its disintegration. The idea of progress, which had such unchallenged power over the mind of Western man for so many decades, has broken down in the world of its origin. It has left behind on the one hand various kinds of totalitarian political fanaticism, and on the other, profound scepticism and disillusionment. There is no reason to doubt and every reason to fear that the inner logic of this idea will work out in the same way in the lands beyond the old Christendom. In other words, it will raise the question, 'What is the destiny of man as such and what, therefore, is the true absolute which must govern his life?'

The world-wide spread of our technological culture and the drawing together of people into a unitary history are, therefore, not religiously neutral events. They are to be understood in relation to the coming of God in Jesus Christ. That coming constitutes the revelation of the true destiny of man and therefore introduces into history for the first time an absolute. As in the immediate ministry of Jesus in the days of his flesh, so also in the continuance of this ministry through the centuries, the coming of this absolute renders neutrality impossible. The coming of this absolute brings men and nations into a position where they must accept it or find another. The universal spread of the secularized form of the Christian eschatology, which is embedded in the technical culture of our day, is in fact drawing nations out of the pools of unhistorical existence and out of the rivulets of tribal history into the single current of world history. And it accords both with the New Testament revelation, and with the facts of our time, to expect that this single world history must increasingly centre around the single issue: Christ or antichrist, the true absolute or its negation.

The figure of antichrist as the symbol of the world's negative decision regarding the absolute claim of Jesus Christ will concern us in a later lecture, after we have considered more fully the meaning of Christ's claim to world dominion. Here my point is simply this: if we take the New Testament as our clue to the interpretation of history, then we shall see the world-wide spread of a single technological culture propelled by the single driving force of a secularized eschatology, as something which is much more than mere scenery for the present stage of the Christian task in the world. We shall see it as part of the process by which all peoples are being brought into that single universal history which is rightly counted from the birth of Christ because it is that history whose meaning and end is finally made known in him. We shall see in the events of our time the operation of the same Lord who in the pages of the Gospels inexorably leads all men to the final issues of life and death—because he is himself the life and the light of the world.

II

WHERE SHALL WE LOOK FOR A WORLD FAITH?

WE have considered briefly the fact that the Western type of scientific civilization has now become a world civilization. The science of the West, its technology, its economics, its law, its political ideas are becoming increasingly the property of mankind as a whole. Obviously in a unified world, such as ours has become, only a world faith has any future. Tribal religion cannot command the loyalty of the men of the modern world, not even if the tribe is as numerous and influential as the tribe of the Western white man. No faith can command a man's final and absolute allegiance, that is to say no faith can be a man's real religion, if he knows that it is only true for certain places and certain people. In a world which knows that there is only one physics and one mathematics, religion cannot do less than claim for its affirmations a like universal validity.

1. *Professor Radhakrishnan's View*

But where is the religion that can make good such a claim? That is our concern in the present lecture. The first answer which falls to be considered is that we should look for this potentially universal religion as the inner essence of the actual religions, or at least of those which we call the higher religions. This is the view which has become almost official dogma in India today, and which is, in effect, the view of many in the Christian Church. There is, of course, a superficial and naïve form of this view which is widely held among those whose

Where Shall We Look?

business involves them with peoples of many faiths. There is, if one may say so, a sort of benevolent polytheism which often appears among the representatives of imperial governments and international business, the kind of polytheism which was tartly described by Gibbon when he said of a certain period in the history of the Roman Empire that all religions were to the people equally true, to the philosophers equally false and to the government equally useful. I remember an occasion when I was a missionary in Kancheepuram during the war. I received a circular from the Government headquarters in the following terms: 'The heads of all temples, mosques and churches are instructed to offer prayer to Almighty God for the success of the allied arms and to report to the Tahsildar's office that they have done so'. One can laugh at this kind of naïve polytheism, a laugh which I hope is not without some sympathy for the poor official who has to keep peace among the various religions. But as far as India is concerned, the view that all religions are in essence the same is based upon foundations much more respectable than mere administrative convenience. It was proclaimed with all the force of a fresh revelation in the teachings of the great Hindu mystic Ramakrishna Paramahamsa. It was restated before the world by his most famous disciple, Swami Vivekananda in his dramatic appearance before the World Parliament of Religions in Chicago, an event which may be said to have marked a new era in the relation of Western thought to Eastern religion. 'The Lord', he said in his address to the Parliament, 'has declared to the Hindu in his incarnation as Krishna, "I am in every religion as the thread through a string of pearls" '.[1] The same view today is expounded with great power and patience by the vice-president of India, Professor Radhakrishnan. He does not claim to be the exponent of one religion among others, but of the real essence within Hinduism, the unchanging truth, which 'is not to be identified with any particular religion, for

[1] *Complete Works of Swami Vivekananda* (Mayavati, Almora, UP: Advaita Ashrama, 1946), 1, 16.

it is the religion which transcends race and creed and yet affirms all races and creeds'. Readers of Dr Radhakrishnan's books will be familiar with the extraordinary skill with which he seeks to show that there is but one essential truth underlying all the religions. If the reader happens also to be familiar with one of the books from which he quarries his material, such as the Bible, he will be astonished to discover how far apparently tough old texts can be stretched to yield new meanings.

But this belief in the one essence of all religions is not merely a matter of the philosopher's chair; it has become very much a matter of national policy. One of the most important things which is happening in India today, I would even say in the world today, is the development of the *Sarvodaya* system of basic education as the standard pattern of elementary education for the greater part of India. A basic school is conceived as a community in which the children learn by sharing in the common tasks of the community. There are no servants, for all must share all the duties, however menial. Learning is centred not in the reading of books, but in the efficient performance of the tasks which the community requires. A great simplicity and austerity are aimed at in regard to material things. And at the centre of the common life is the corporate act of common worship, early in the morning and at sunset, which is regarded as the indispensable focus of the community's life. It takes the form of prayers and meditations drawn from the sacred books and traditions of all the religions. The names of Ram, Jesus, Allah, Buddha, etc., are used indifferently. Every effort is made to adapt the form of worship to the beliefs of those taking part, so that it may be an effective focus for the whole common life. The significance of this remarkable development will be seen when it is added that these basic schools are regarded as the nurseries for the kind of co-operative village communities which will develop with the development of the *Gramdan* movement. The word *Gramdan* means the gift of a village and is a development of

Where Shall We Look? 33

the earlier *Bhoodan* or gift of land. Gramdan means that all private land in a village is surrendered so that it may become the common property of the whole and be managed co-operatively for the common good. For this kind of community living, the basic schools are the nurseries, and at the very heart of them stands the form of common worship which I have described, the expression of what is believed to be the true essence of religion in which men of all kinds can find their unity. Here then is perhaps the most impressive attempt which has yet been seen to find a common faith for mankind and to make it, not merely in theory but in practice, the basis for a common life. At the present time, the eyes of those who are engaged in this *Sarvodaya* movement are fixed upon the needs of India, but undoubtedly many of them would claim that they have here something not only for India, but for the world, a world faith answering to the needs of the coming world civilization. I hope I have said enough to indicate that it is a claim which we should consider with the greatest seriousness.

If one ventures to examine this claim, one can only do so with a profound respect for the integrity and self-sacrifice of those who are making it. One could begin by speaking of certain elementary, practical difficulties which, however, lead us to more fundamental, theoretical questions. How far, for instance, can the principle of democracy be carried in the sphere of religion? A friend of mine was a member of a *Sarvodaya* community of the kind which I have described, in which, as elsewhere, the Lord's prayer was used for common worship. One member of the group expressed his difficulties with the phrase 'forgive us our trespasses' which did not, he felt, correspond with any reality in his own experience. The problem was brought up for discussion in the whole group, as the result of which my friend as the only Christian was very courteously requested to bring back a revised draft of the prayer. He had difficulty in explaining his inability to do so. The idea of something absolutely given, a *datum* in religion, threatened to disrupt a fellowship based on the principle of agreement by discussion and sharing.

But perhaps that is not quite a fair statement of the issue. Obviously the principle that nothing is given cannot be absolutized. Even a basic school would not accept the majority vote of the pupils in the third form to revise Boyle's law or rescind the theorem of Pythagoras. Some things must be accepted as given, and religion cannot be made an exception to that rule without destroying its claim to truth. But, it would be replied, we do not teach Boyle's law as something to be accepted on the mere authority of the teacher or of Dr Boyle. We know that it can be verified in experience, if the pupils have the time and patience and knowledge to do it. The truths of religion are likewise to be verified in experience. That is a valid reply. And it points to the fact that the dogma that all religions are in essence the same is not a mere abandonment of any concern for truth. It is a dogma based upon experience and believed to be capable of experimental verification. Underneath the religious democracy of a *Sarvodaya* community, there is a solid foundation of religious dogma based upon religious experience. Our task is to examine that foundation. The appearance of benevolence and openheartedness which naturally attaches to a proposal to treat all religions as essentially the same is superficial and ought not to deceive us. It may of course spring from mere indifference to truth; it may spring from a belief that the things which religion talks about do not exist, and that it is therefore a waste of time to argue about them; or, and this I am convinced is the truth in this case, it may spring from a belief that there is a reality which underlies the differing expressions of religion and which is the real truth within them. Probably all these three states of mind can be discovered in India as elsewhere. But what we are dealing with in the teachings of Ramakrishna, Vivekananda, and Radhakrishnan certainly belongs to the third category. What Dr Radhakrishnan called 'the religion which transcends race and creed, yet informs all races and creeds' is a definite religion

Where Shall We Look?

which has to be examined on its merits. Like every true religion, it claims, it must claim, to illuminate all truth and to interpret all experience. Christianity does the same. But this claim does not excuse it from the necessity of being examined, its claim to truth tested, its foundation in experience exposed. That is what we must now do.

If we examine the writings of Radhakrishnan we are left in no doubt as to where the foundation lies. It lies in the tradition of mystical experience of which India has been the greatest and most resolute exponent. This is where Ramakrishna Paramahamsa himself received his assurance of the essential identity of all religions. And it is in the experience of the mystics that modern writers like Radhakrishnan find the ground for their certitude that there is a common essence within all religions.

Dr Radhakrishnan writes as follows:

> The Hindu attitude (to other religions) is based upon a definite philosophy of life, which assumes that religion is a matter of personal realization... Spirit is free being, and its life consists in breaking free from conventions and penetrating into true being. The formless blaze of spiritual life cannot be expressed in human words. We tread on air so thin and rare that we do not leave any visible footprints. He who has seen the real is lifted above all narrowness, relativities and contingencies.[1]

This inability to express the real in human words does not, however, as Radhakrishnan makes very clear, mean that there is anything vague about it. The basis of the Hindu position, as he says, is a very definite philosophy, which, like other philosophies, is capable of statement and of criticism and which, in turn, is based upon an experience which is described as 'personal realization', 'penetration into true being', 'seeing the real'. That philosophy is what India calls the 'Vedanta', the end and summation of all revelation. It teaches that the

[1] S. Radhakrishnan, *Eastern Religions and Western Thought* (London: Oxford University Press, 1939) pp. 316-17.

reality behind all the manifold appearance and all the ceaseless change which our five senses report to us is one undifferentiated and unchanging spirit and that that spirit is identical with our own spirit. That spirit is defined as 'pure awareness distinct from bodily states and mental happenings',[1] And, as the repeated refrain of the Chandogya Upanishad expresses it, 'This whole world has that being for itself—that is reality—that is the self—that art thou O Svetaketu'.[2]

This pure awareness, however, this naked condition of pure selfhood, is normally beyond our power to realize. In proportion as we depart from it, the world takes on an appearance of multiplicity and diversity. And not only so, the experience of pure selfhood which was present in the moment of mystical union now appears in our memory as something different from our empirical self (which, indeed, it is) and to that something we give the name of 'God'. To quote Radhakrishnan again: 'The attainment of spiritual status when refracted in the logical universe appears as a revelation of grace'.[3]

Thus for the Vedantin the whole conception of divine revelation belongs, along with the visible and tangible world, to the realm of *maya*. Modern Hindu writes are anxious to insist that the doctrine of *maya* does not mean that the phenomenal world is illusory. It does teach, however, that the appearance of multiplicity and change is illusory. For the Vedantin, the final truth is contained in the sentences which we have quoted from the Chandogya Upanishad, 'Thou art that'. Pure selfhood is the ultimate reality at the heart of all existence. 'Our real self is the supreme being'.[4] The apparent differences between things, and even the difference between subject and object, are transcended when the self understands its true nature. The phenomenal world cannot, according to the *maya* doctrine, be dismissed as non-existent. In so far as it is a refraction of the one reality seen through the eyes of the self which does not understand true selfhood, it is real; but its ap-

[1] *Ibid.*, p. 122.
[2] Chandogya Upanishad VI. 10.
[3] Radhakrishnan, *op. cit.*, p. 29.
[4] *Ibid.*, p. 32.

Where Shall We Look?

pearance of diversity, multiplicity, and change is unreal. 'So long as we are in the world of *maya* and occupy a dualistic standpoint, the world is there standing over against us determining our perceptions and conduct.'[1] So Radhakrishnan paraphrases the teachings of Sankaracharya. Thus, so long as we are living in the world of illusion, the illusions are real to us. But this is precisely the character of all illusion. And the whole idea of divine revelation belongs to this world of illusion. The reality of which it is the refraction is none other than the mystical experience of unity with the supreme soul, which is the self.

The ultimate basis of the whole Hindu position is thus the experience of mystical union with the ultimate. On this Radhakrishnan is very explicit: 'The religions of the world can be distinguished into those which emphasize the object and those which insist on experience. For the first class, religion is an attitude of faith and conduct, directed to a power without. For the second, it is an experience to which the individual attaches supreme value. The Hindu and the Buddist religions are of this class.'[2] That experience has been described many times by mystics, East and West, and the essential features of their description are the same. The essence of it is, first, a gradual withdrawal of the mind from the world of sense perception by exercise in ascetic discipline; second, the concentration of all the mental powers upon a single object, upon an image, a text, upon a single sound, such as the sacred syllable 'om', or upon some part of the body, until the soul becomes empty of everything except the object of its meditation; and finally, the point is reached where even the object of meditation ceases to be an object distinct from the subject. Subject and object are dissolved in a single unitary awareness, which is not an apprehension of any object but only, if one may put it so, awareness in an intransitive sense. 'The soul, holding itself in emptiness, finds itself possessing all.' And those who have visited these sublime heights tell us that they have ex-

[1] *Ibid.*, p. 87. [2] *Ibid.*, p. 21.

perienced a rapture beyond any earthly joy, a knowledge beyond logic, a peace beyond understanding.

It is that experience which provides the basis of certitude upon which the Hindu attitude to other religions rests. From that standpoint, every expression of the religious sense, whether it be the most primitive idolatry or the most refined and spiritual theism, is seen to be but a refraction of the one ultimate truth seen through human natures which are at various stages of development—that is to say, at various stages of liberation from the toils of *maya*. Within such a view of reality, there is room for almost infinite tolerance. Human nature varies, and each man is free to join the stream of living religion at the place to which his nature and environment lead him. There is no place for mutual criticism or hostility. Each man must be encouraged to be faithful to the religious path of his choice but, at the same time, to penetrate behind the forms of religion, its alleged revelations, its creeds and dogmas and rituals, to find through them (and it does not matter what they are) the one truth, which is not a dogmatic statement or a personal meeting but an experience of identity with the Supreme Being.

The one thing which on this view cannot be tolerated is the assertion which Christianity is bound to make, namely, that the Supreme Being has, once and for all, revealed himself in a historic person; that truth is to be found only by relating one's self to him; and that he is the centre around which the unity of mankind here in history is to be built. To such a claim, when it is clearly understood, Hinduism, in obedience to its own fundamental tenets, can only present an unrelenting opposition. From the point of view of the Vedanta, the preaching of the Christian gospel is an assertion of ultimate validity for something which belongs to the world of illusion. If the preacher does it in ignorance, he may be gently and patiently helped to see beyond his illusion to the reality which he has not yet understood. But if he does it knowing what he is doing and if he steadily refuses to accept the view of his

Where Shall We Look?

own faith which Hinduism offers him, then the limits of Hindu tolerance are necessarily reached. No tolerance can be infinite. It must be intolerant of intolerance, and when that tragic situation is forced upon us, we cannot help facing the question of truth. Is the Hindu view of religion true, and can it provide the means of unity for mankind?

There is no need to doubt, and it would be impertinence to doubt, the reality of the mystic experience. But when the mystic builds upon his experience a philosophy and a theology, the matter is open for debate. I have no special competence to take part in that debate, but this comment at least may be pardoned; the Hindu mystic begins by abstracting himself from all apprehensions of phenomena. It is therefore only to be expected that he ends with a state of pure unitary awareness, undisturbed by any kind of multiplicity. He has what he set out to seek. From the standpoint he has taken, all multiplicity has ceased to exist, because he has deliberately shut it out of his attention. But to conclude that this experience is the clue to ultimate reality is not a logical deduction, but a leap of faith; for the whole question is: What is the relation of that ultimate reality to the multiplicity of phenomena? We face here, surely, an ultimate decision, which is, in the last resort, a decision of faith: whether we regard the multiplicity and change which characterize human life as a mere veil which has to be torn away in order that we may have access to ultimate reality, or whether we regard them as the place where we are to meet with and know and serve the divine purpose; whether salvation is by absorption into the Supreme Being, conceived as undifferentiated and unchanging spirit abstracted from all contact with phenomena, or whether it is by reconciliation to the Supreme Being, conceived as personal will active in and through phenomena. Here is the dividing line between all religions; and the main tradition of Hinduism stands fair and square on one side of it. The claim that the Vedanta is the truth transcending all religions is necessarily a flat denial of the central truth of biblical religion. The reality of the mystical experience need not be denied and, indeed, cannot be; but the assertion that it is the clue to reality is an affirmation of faith which must be judged by the criteria that are proper in the field of religious belief.

It follows from the nature of this basic experience that the unity which Hinduism offers is rather the negative unity of tolerance than the positive unity of love. Hinduism is a way of salvation for the individual. Radhakrishnan, after describing the varieties of Hindu theological thought, adds: 'All, however, are agreed in regarding salvation as the attainment of the true status of the individual. Belief and conduct, rites and ceremonies, authorities and dogma, are assigned to a place subordinate to the art of conscious self-discovery and contact with the divine.' Hinduism has no doctrine of the Church. By its essential character, it bids men seek beyond all the visible forms which are the mark of any human community. The standpoint from which it views all religions is the standpoint of the experience of unity with the supreme self, and that standpoint is necessarily a purely individual experience. There can be no such thing as a corporate *samadhi*. Nor can the individual experience lead out consistently into a corporate expression. It produces an almost infinite tolerance and courtesy to all other faiths and an abhorrence of all religious strife and bigotry. But it would be quite contrary to its own nature to produce a historic community bound together by fixed rules and customs. Modern Hinduism is largely the faith of men who have been educated in the Christian schools and colleges or at least in a medium full of Christian ideas; men who know their Bibles better than many Christians do; men who have learned to love and reverence Jesus and his teachings. Their writings are, therefore, full of Christian phraseology, and their activities are often profoundly influenced by Christian ideas. But so long as the central and controlling idea is salvation through the knowledge of identity with the Supreme Self, so long as the world of multiplicity and change is believed to be unreal, Hinduism can never put a visible human community into the centre of its creed, as Christianity puts the church. The unity which it offers is the cessation of strife, not the creation of a new community.

Thus the Hindu offer of reconciliation between religions is a consistent whole from start to finish. It begins with the assumption with which it ends, namely, that the phenomenal world of multiplicity and change is illusory. It therefore begins by a process of withdrawal from that world, and it ends with a conception of salvation which can have no organic relation to any particular historic events or to any visible historic community. Its claim to be the truth transcending all religions is necessarily at the same time a negation of the truth of those religions as their adherents understand them. So far from providing the basis for a permanent truce between the religions, it is—when properly understood—a declaration of war upon all religion which claims to be based upon a historic revelation.

2. Professor Toynbee's View

In our search for a world faith, we turn next to look briefly at the recent writings of one of the most distinguished of living historians. I refer to the lectures given recently in Harvard University by Professor Toynbee. He begins by considering criteria for comparison among the religions and suggests what are the weaker and stronger points among them. He looks at the rise of the modern world civilization and at the relation of Christianity to it. He concludes that the great enemy that faces man is the worship of collective man, of Leviathan, and he pleads 'that all the higher living religions ought to subordinate their traditional rivalries and make a new approach to one another in face of a fearful common adversary'.[1] This requires, he says, that Christianity should purge itself firstly of its westernism and secondly of its traditional belief that Christianity is unique, a belief which inevitably produces intolerance and pride.[2]

[1] A. J. Toynbee, *Christianity among the Religions of the World* (London: Oxford University Press, 1958), p. 85.   [2] Pp. 92 ff.

When a man like Professor Toynbee, writing with such immense learning and in such a Christian spirit, warns us against the pride and exclusiveness of Christians, I think we have to listen attentively and penitently. And yet, I must humbly say that it does not seem to me that Professor Toynbee has sufficiently examined his own presuppositions. In the first place, although he sets out to speak of criteria for making comparison among the religions, he never states what is the basis upon which he makes his assessment of the value of the religions, nor indicates that the question has ever occurred to him. Of course, we can compare religions in a purely relative way; that is to say we can simply say that Buddhism teaches this whereas Islam teaches that. But Professor Toynbee does much more than this: he evaluates the religions, he praises some elements in them and deplores others, he regards some religions as higher and others as lower. But he never indicates where he finds the scale by which to make these measurements, never even indicates that the question has occurred to him. In fact, he quietly takes it for granted that his own standard of ethical values is shared by his readers and requires no examination. In the light of it, he judges all the religions and finds Christianity itself defective because by its claim to an exclusive revelation it has inevitably nurtured the sin of pride.

My first comment on this is merely preliminary. It is true, alas, that Christians have often been guilty of pride and intolerance. But pride is not an inevitable concomitant of a belief in the uniqueness of Christianity. If I believe that God really did send his Son into the world to die for me and all men, I am bound to say that that message is incomparable and final. And if I understand it rightly, it means the end of all my pride. It means that I am a debtor with an unpayable debt to pay to my Lord, which he has bidden me discharge by loving my neighbour. There have been proud and intolerant Christians, but the gospel has surely proved its power to make proud men humble. Pride is not inevitably involved in

Where Shall We Look? 43

the attitude of the man who confesses that Christ alone is saviour. It would be more plausible to argue that an element of pride is inevitably involved if, in the strength of one's own unexamined ethical perceptions, one passes judgments among the great religions of the world, declaring some to be higher and others lower. It would be interesting to hear a comment on Professor Toynbee's argument at this point from an adherent of one of the religions which he regards as lower.

My second comment is more fundamental. When we talk about religion, it is generally understood that we are talking about man's belief and practices in regard to what he thinks to be final and determinative, the final reality of life. A man's religion is, properly speaking, what has right of way over every other thing including even life itself. When a religious man, therefore, meets another religion, he is bound to evaluate the latter in the light of his own. Hinduism has its own interpretation of Christianity and Islam and the other religions. So has Islam. So has Christianity. But when Professor Toynbee claims to judge among the religions and to evaluate them in the light of his judgments of goodness and truth, what is his standpoint? Either he is judging them as a Christian, in which case his judgment is not impartial; or else he is claiming a standpoint above all religions, which would mean that he represents a truer and higher religion than any of the existing ones. If that were so, we would need an exposition of this religion and of its basis in history and experience. But I do not think that Professor Toynbee would claim this. He would recognize, I think, that man has no vantage point above the religions from which he can judge them. I think that he would say that he is really judging them as a Christian. But he adds that Christianity itself must purge itself of its exclusiveness and recognize that its own central ideas are also present in the other higher religions, higher that is to say from the point of view of Christianity.

But these two demands, that Christianity should shed its exclusiveness and recognize the presence of its central idea in other religions, really bring us to the heart of our question. What are Christianity's central ideas? Professor Toynbee has defined them as three: that God loves his creatures to the point of self-sacrifice, that man ought to share that love, and that they should put it into practice.[1] He then goes on to point out that these three ideas are present also in other religions, and that even the idea of the divine self-sacrifice, which is so central in Christianity, is to be found in various other religions. Let us accept these statements as they stand for a moment. If we accept them, the question has then to be asked: what is our evidence for the belief that these ideas are true? How do we know that they are not just ancient and hoary illusions? In the face of all the overwhelming evidence to the contrary, what is our ground for believing that the creator and controller of this whole sum of things is really motivated by nothing but self-sacrificing love for his creatures? It is not obvious. I submit, as a Christian, that the only ground I know is what may be called the total fact of Christ. The idea which Professor Toynbee rightly regards as central to Christianity is not an induction which can be derived from general human experience. The man who is wrestling with this tough fellow the world, as Luther called it, wants to know what basis there is in fact for this idea. The only basis I know is what I have called the total fact of Christ, by which I mean that the man Jesus, being what the New Testament testifies him to be, and knowing, as St John says, that he came from God and went to God, died and rose again. Professor Toynbee does not mention the resurrection. I do not know whether it fits into his scheme. But I submit that it is a matter of well-attested fact that the Christian faith about God was launched upon the world in the power of the resurrection belief, and that it is the reasonable inference from such record as we have that apart from the resurrection, the preceding story of the life and death of Jesus would not have produced what we call the Christian faith. If it is true, as Christians

[1] *Ibid.*, p. 106.

believe, that it did really happen, that Almighty God came down on earth to die for our sins and to rise again for our justification, then we can understand the effects in history, and the present world-wide spread, of the idea that God loved the world. We can also understand, since God has not left himself without a witness at any time, that men have always been haunted by the thought that sacrificial love was the greatest reality. And the Christian must surely welcome these thoughts wherever he finds them. But if it suggested, as it is by Professor Toynbee, that he rid himself of the idea that in his message about Jesus he has a unique and final and decisive message for the world, then we must answer that this is asking him to destroy the only basis for the common platform upon which Professor Toynbee wants him to stand alongside the other higher religions.

But this leads on to a further point. Professor Toynbee sees Christianity as essentially an idea of God and a code of conduct corresponding to it, and he naturally wants to see more co-operation among those who hold the same ideas. We must certainly agree that all people, whether religious or not, should co-operate so far as they can irrespective of creed to do the things that the welfare of man requires. But at the heart of Christianity, it has surely always been understood that there is not a system of ideas, not even simply a code of conduct, but an announcement of events. Christianity is primarily news and only secondarily views. It is not an ideology. Above all, it is not an anti-communist or anti-fascist or anti-totalitarian ideology. Here, I must frankly confess that I find Professor Toynbee's suggestion horrifying. If anything would qualify for being decorated with the overworked adjective demonic, it would be an alliance of religions to combat nationalism and communism. We have surely already enough evidence to show what happens when religion is used, I say used, for that kind of purpose. Christianity, at least, cannot submit to that treatment. Surely it is not irrelevant that the early Christians were called atheists. That was not a complete misunderstanding.

They did not believe that the things which men called gods exist. Christianity exists not to propagate ideas but to testify to the acts of God, acts which judge the Church as they judge the world. By holding fast to its testimony to these acts, to what I have called the total fact of Christ, the church will be guarded against the sin of absolutizing itself and so becoming guilty of blind pride. Basing its faith not on its own ideas but on God's acts, it will be prepared to recognize that even in secularist and anti-religious movements the living God may be at work, both to build up and to destroy; and to recognize also that religion itself may become the stronghold of evil powers, which the living God will unmask and destroy even by the hands of godless men.

What, in the last analysis, is the antidote to man's worship of himself? It is not, I submit, man's religion, even if that religion is the summation of all man's highest thoughts about God. Such an alliance of the so-called higher religions of mankind, if it were possible, would be the final form of man's self-worship. The only thing that can finally humble mankind is an act of God his creator. The Christian message is that God has performed such an act, an act of utter self-abasement for man's sake. The Christian can make no exclusive claims for himself, but he must make an exclusive claim for that act, for the total fact of Christ, as providing the only point at which the final issues of human life are exposed and settled.

3. *Professor Hocking's View*

As a third line of search for the universal faith, I venture to refer to a recent book by a very distinguished teacher of Harvard University, Professor Hocking's book, *The Coming World Civilization*. The first part of this book contains a brilliant and fascinating study of the relations between Christianity and the technological civilization which it has begotten, and which Professor Hocking believes is now an independent entity no longer dependent upon its parent for spiritual sustenance. He then comes to the crucial question which concerns us in this

Where Shall We Look? 47

lecture, namely, where are we to find a world faith to match this world civilization? He concludes that Christianity can provide that faith on two conditions—that it comes to terms with its own offspring in its own house, and that it shows itself to be universal and not merely Western, as universal as technology has become. In asking that Christianity become universal, Professor Hocking is not asking it to shed its history. He convincingly demonstrates that this is impossible for 'it belongs to the essence of Christianity that its world view is being actualized in history'. But the history is emphatically the history of man's appropriation of the idea, not the history of the idea itself. 'The vision of the eternal, *not the eternal itself*, must have its history.'[1] Therefore, while we can neither discard history nor overleap it, we can look forward to a time when the particular names and places associated with man's vision of the eternal can be, if not forgotten, at least removed from a position of absolute significance. We can look to a confluence of the great religions, the result not of an easygoing relativism, for Professor Hocking does not advocate that, but the result of a spiritual struggle in which even an element of fanaticism may have its proper place, a struggle of free wills to actualize in history an order of being congruent with the faith that the ultimate nature of things is suffering love. But in the end, the Christian will not insist upon the specific name of Jesus. The saying 'He who loses his life for my sake shall find it' applies to Christianity itself. In a moving question, Professor Hocking hints at rather than states his final answer. 'If Jumna and Ganges run together, shall the united lower stream be called Ganges or Jumna? Is it neither? Is it both? Or is it that one whose symbol men freely find compacted with the sense of both, holding in a historic life and deed, for which there can be no repetition and no substitute, a prophetic answer to man's eternal need'?[1] This haunting question is the nearest that Professor Hocking comes to an

[1] W. E. Hocking, *The Coming World Civilization* (London: Allen and Unwin, 1958), p. 85. [2] *Ibid.*, p. 170.

assertion of the finality of the gospel. But it is a far cry from this to the ringing affirmation of Peter before the Jewish Sanhedrin: 'There is none other name given under heaven whereby you must be saved'.

On which side of this wide gulf does the truth lie? Let me simply make three comments.

(a) As between Professor Hocking and the Bible, I think we are dealing with two radically different conceptions of the meaning of the word 'faith'. For him, it is axiomatic that faith is an individual experience of timeless reality. 'The clean aloneness of the subjective I-am, free from social involvement, must be the starting point of all religious experience, the measure of its depth and vitality.'[1] The individual, and the history of his apprehension of the eternal as love, this is the centre of the picture for Professor Hocking. For the Bible it is wholly otherwise; the centre of the picture is occupied by the living God who calls a people to himself. Here two points are involved, first the initiative of God and second the fundamentally social character of religion. In the Bible, the eternal emphatically *has a history*, however shocking it may be to the philosopher. God does things, now one thing, now another. He promises, he warns, he threatens, he does new things, he announces them beforehand. The centre of the stage is occupied from cover to cover of the Bible by the living God who creates and destroys, who calls and pleads and wrestles with his people, who besets them behind and before, who follows them even down to Sheol, who blocks up their pathways to turn them into the way of righteousness, who spreads out his hands to a disobedient and gainsaying people. In Professor Hocking's writings I find no trace of this at all. This masterful, living, sovereign Lord is never seen. Only faint and muffled echoes of his voice are heard. He is Love, but he can give no sign of it for he is not allowed to have a history. This mighty, masterful Lover of the Bible has only the name of love left to him but not its nature. And correspondingly, the Bible regards

[1] *Ibid.*, p. 73.

Where Shall We Look?

the faith of the individual as secondary and not primary. The primary fact is that God has called the people to himself to be his people, to know him, to be with him, to be his witnesses. This is so both in the Old Testament and in the New. 'You did not choose me, but I chose you', says the Lord to his people. The beginning of faith for Peter and Andrew and James and John was not the clean aloneness of the subjective I-am; it was social from the beginning.

(b) It is very easy to understand that from the starting point which he adopts, Professor Hocking can find no permanent or absolute place for the name of Jesus. 'The concept of the Christ', he says, must be 'extended to include that unbound Spirit who stands and has stood at the door of every man, and who in various guises, still appears to him who opens, both as impersonal word and as personal presence'.[1] And again, 'the faith of the Christian is continuous with the mature faith by which all men live—the light that at least dimly "lighteth every man that cometh into the world". It is the making fully explicit of this universal faith: it is therefore present in some degree wherever religion is present'.[2] Here the logical fallacy is surely obvious. The only proper deduction from the Johannine statement concerning the light that lighteth every man is that it is present wherever *man* is present, not wherever *religion* is present. There is nothing in the text to justify a reference to religion. The religion which Professor Hocking identifies with the light includes what the Bible identifies with darkness. That is why we find that it is the irreligious of the New Testament, the publicans and harlots, who go into the kingdom, while the religious identify themselves with the powers of darkness and become the murderers of Jesus.

But we must surely go further and say that to speak of a 'Christ concept' which could be detached from the figure of Jesus of Nazareth would be, in the perspective of the Bible, unbelief. Before the coming of Jesus, the word 'Christ' stood for a concept which was still plastic. The Christian faith is

[1] *Ibid.*, pp. 168-9 [2] *Ibid.*, p. 113.

that Jesus is the Christ. And for those who accept this, the word Christ no longer denotes a plastic idea; it denotes the man Jesus whose life and death and resurrection are recorded in the New Testament. To believe, in the language of the New Testament, is to believe *that*. It is to believe that in this actual historic figure and in these events God's kingdom and God's Christ are present. Jesus is the Christ: that is the fundamental faith of the New Testament. To insist upon this is not religious bigotry but fidelity to the facts of human nature. If the word Christ is a plastic term whose meaning depends only upon the accumulated religious experience of a multitude of lone individuals in their search for reality, then we are left finally imprisoned in our own subjectivity. But if the living God, the only true 'I am', has actually confronted us with his own personal presence in Jesus, we are then truly delivered into a new dimension of existence whose centre is not our faith but his acts and words. On the question whether the word Christ is or is not indissolubly and finally riveted to the name of Jesus hangs the whole issue between life and death for man.

(c) Professor Hocking has a very interesting section in which he contends for the necessity of the historical in religion. Christianity as a philosophic teaching might, he says, have separated itself from the accidents of its history; but Christianity as a faith committed to the task of getting God's will done in the world could not do so. The idea of love lacks an essential element of perfection if it is not being incarnated in actual lives and deeds. Thus Christianity cannot exist in the world as pure idea, but must be involved in a concrete historic community. You cannot universalize Christianity by disembodying it, for that would be to rob it of an essential element. Yet at the same time, 'the particular aspects of such a historical movement (as Christianity) are in constant tension with its universal character'[1] and this tension is perpetually renewed. In other words, the universal in (for ex-

[1] *Ibid.*, p. 125.

ample) Christianity cannot be separated from the concrete and historical, but neither can it be identified with it.

This is well argued, but the argument stops short of the crucial issue. In so far as it refers to the history of the Christian Church, a Christian—at least if he is a Protestant—can accept it entirely. But the crucial question is whether the argument is to include also the historic events which are the objects of the Church's faith—namely the events of the Incarnation. It is the faith of Christians that at one point in human history the universal and the concrete historical completely coincided, that the Man Jesus was the incarnate Word of God, that in his works and words the perfect will of God was done without defect or remainder. The complete fusion of the idea and the deed at this point in world history is the whole essence of Christianity, and if they are pulled apart there is no Gospel to preach. It is because of what I have called the total fact of Christ that the idea of Christianity is credible. If it be a fact that in Jesus the God who created all things, the Lord of glory, humbled himself to die as a criminal for the sin of the world, and that having died he rose again as victor over death, then it is possible to believe and to preach that—in spite of all appearances to the contrary—love rules the world. But the truth of the preaching stands or falls with the truth of the report concerning Jesus, and that report must remain the central content of the preaching. But if— on the other hand—the story of Jesus is only one of the particular historic illustrations or concretions of a general religious truth which is available to men on other grounds, then certainly one can agree to drop that name in the interests of a wider harmony. But then two questions arise: firstly, what are the other grounds on which it is believed that love rules the world? and secondly, is the implied view of Jesus compatible with the record?

On the first point, Professor Hocking appeals to a universal mystical experience in the human race. The reality of this experience cannot be denied. The interpretation of it is open for discussion. There is surely overwhelming evidence to show that the cultivation of pure mysticism, apart from the influence of the historic revelation in Jesus Christ, leads eventually to a total pessimism about the world and to the development of religious practices designed to free the soul altogether from entanglement in the processes of history. I must simply say that I do not know of grounds apart from Christ upon which it is possible to build a strong and enduring faith that self-sacrificing love is really the sovereign power that rules the world. I have not yet met anyone who could show them.

The second question requires us to go to the only available record of the words and works of Jesus, and to ask whether the view that Jesus is but one illustration and concretion of a general religious truth available on other grounds tallies with the facts. It seems to me that it does not. Jesus plainly regarded his own coming as an event of decisive significance for mankind. In his parable of the vineyard he identifies himself as the one in whom God's final and decisive claim is made. Before the High Priest he accepts the identification of himself with the Son of Man whom Daniel had seen coming with the clouds of heaven. He tells his disciples that to acknowledge or deny him before men means being acknowledged or denied before God, and that he alone knows the Father and can give that knowledge to others. He tells them that to die for him means being assured of life. In the face of these and other similar sayings which disclose his own thought about himself, the old alternative *aut Deus aut non bonus*[1] becomes inescapable. If these words of his are true, then he is no mere exemplar of a general principle, but is himself the one in whom God is present to deal personally and decisively with his people; if they are not true then he is deceived and a deceiver, and it were better that his name be forgotten lest it should deceive generations yet to come. Certainly there can be no doubt about the position of the New Testament on this

[1] i.e., that Jesus was either God or not a good man.

Where Shall We Look?

issue. The apostolic faith is not a faith of which Jesus was one of the teachers and exemplars; it is faith in Jesus. The end to which the apostolic writers looked was that at the Name of Jesus every knee should bow and every tongue confess him Lord to the glory of God the Father.

4. *A Unique Revelation?*

Can we of the twentieth century still believe that this faith, centred in the Name of *one* of the world's great religious figures, can be the universal faith for mankind? If we do so believe, are we merely betraying our inability to rise above the limitations of our own tradition? I answer that question by putting another: when we look for a universal faith for mankind, what are we expecting to find? Are we expecting to find something so wholly free from the taint of locality that it has already occurred to everybody everywhere? Obviously not. Are we then looking for an idea which is universal in the sense that once it is expounded it is obvious to all men, such as the laws of science, about which it does not matter much when or where they were discovered, for once they are explained they are obvious to all? But alas, we know well that the possession of a common corpus of scientific knowledge does not unite us. We might even reach a point at which science had created a universally agreed picture of how a scientifically controlled world should be planned. But the question who is finally to plan whom would still torment and divide us, a question which lies outside the calculus of science. Are we then looking for a common mystical experience where we could find a harmony beneath all the multiplicity and movement of this world? Such a harmony would certainly in principle destroy the aggressive will that causes us to seek to dominate one another. But it would equally destroy in the long run the will to create an ordered world. The final effect of pure acosmic mysticism is not to effect a real harmony within the world of history but merely to place a minus sign outside the bracket in which the daily life of mankind has to be lived. It does not change the relation of the terms within the bracket.

What then are we seeking? Surely what we seek is a harmony of wills in which our several wills without being destroyed are redeemed from their natural egotism and brought into co-operation. We seek reconciliation, and we know that without it we shall certainly destroy one another. But reconciliation can only come from a new birth of love in men's hearts, and love cannot be begotten out of fear. The very reiteration of our need for unity, and of the appalling horrors that will attend our failure to find it, strengthens all those self-regarding elements which are the enemy of love. Only love can beget love. But how shall love be found? It is not in man. We must ask it of God. But how shall God show his love if not by deeds? And if they are deeds, they have a date and place. Is it irrational then to look to particular and local events as the possible source of a universal faith? Rather, it would surely be irrational to refuse so to look.

Our dilemma can be defined yet more sharply. We seek peace, a lasting peace but also a righteous peace. We know that peace cannot be had by mere appeasement at the cost of righteousness; and we know, or we ought to know by now, that when we say above all things 'We will have righteousness', it also eludes us, for our righteousness either national or personal becomes self-righteousness. How can we find a peace which does not become mere appeasement and a righteousness that does not become self-righteousness? Only at the place where there is a holy forgiveness, which means the forgiveness of God against whom men have sinned and who is our judge. The place where righteousness and peace have kissed each other must be provided by God who alone can forgive sin. That place must be somewhere, for forgiveness is an act that must have a date and place. It is, I repeat, not irrational to believe that the human family might find its unity not everywhere or anywhere, not wherever each of us chooses, but at the place which God has provided—if he has

Where Shall We Look?

provided—a mercy seat where sin is judged and pardoned.

And here, I must, so to speak, stop, and continue in a different way. We have talked about man's quest for unity. All that I have said leads simply to this point: man cannot find it, God must give it. Like Job and his friends, we have to stop talking and listen because God has spoken. The roles are suddenly reversed. When you pick up a Bible in the midst of a discussion such as we have had, it is as though you have suddenly to turn around and face the other way. The questions you were asking die on your lips. For you realize that you are now the one who is questioned. The programme is after all not in your hands but in those of another, and the question is, are you ready for all that it involves? Not that you are swept off your feet; certainly not. You are required to stand and answer. But it is a much more tremendous question even than you had realized. It is not just a matter of life and death; it is a message from beyond death. The dying and rising of Jesus constitutes an event beside which even the future existence of human civilization is a secondary question. The Christian claim is that that event has to be announced to the whole world as the one secret of reconciliation first between man and his Maker and second between man and man. I hope to have shown reason why this claim should not be dismissed as a piece of provincialism intruding itself into a universal debate. To explore the nature and content of that claim will be our business in the two ensuing lectures.

III

BY WHAT AUTHORITY?
THE PRESUPPOSITIONS OF CHRIST'S
REVELATION

WE have now looked at some of the proposals which have been made in the direction of a world faith, answering to the needs of the one world civilization of our day. We saw reasons for the belief that it is not irrational or merely narrow-minded to look for the source of such a universal faith in a series of particular events. We looked at the Christian claim to have in fact a message which is to be preached to the whole world and which offers the hope of human unity. We saw that the authority of that message does not lie in its promise of unifying mankind but rather in its source, in its origin. And we must now consider that point further.

Christian missions have been constantly callenged to answer the question 'By what authority do you do this?' It is asked by the man in India today who stops in the street to hear an evangelist preaching and inquiries indignantly whether he does not know that the lease of this foreign religion has run out. It is asked by Christians in the churches of the West. And Christian missions themselves have constantly been guilty of giving the wrong answer. A study of the history of the promotional literature of Christian missions would produce some strange results. They have been advocated as providing the crown of Western culture, as a sort of spiritual cement for the British Empire, as the religious counterpart of the democratic way of life, and as an antidote to world communism. We have learned to laugh at most of these by now,

The Presuppositions of Christ's Revelation

though the last is still sometimes heard. We ought to have learned by now, that these alliances do us no good. Even to advocate Christian missions as the answer to the problems of a divided world is to confuse the issues. If the question 'By what authority?' is pressed, then there is only one answer possible and it must be given as plainly as possible. It is the answer which the earliest missionaries gave when they were asked: 'In the name of Jesus'. That is the only answer which does not confound the issues because it brings the questioner face to face with the one real issue with which the mission is concerned, namely the person of Jesus himself. It is Jesus himself who presents mankind with its only real crisis and who raises for the whole human race the question beside which even the survival of human civilization is a secondary question.

The Christian missionary has nothing to do but to bring men face to face with Jesus Christ, the total fact of Jesus. The only authority to which he can appeal is the authority of Jesus Christ. Now to say that is, of course, to say that Jesus is himself the ultimate authority for mankind, an authority not requiring to be ratified by any other. And that is, in fact, the Christian claim, a claim that goes back to Jesus himself as we see him in the gospels. The gospel record shows that the question of authority arose from the very beginning. Men noticed that he spoke with authority and not as the scribes. We know how the scribes spoke; they spoke from the authorities. They claimed no ultimate authority of their own but they rested their teaching on prior authority. Jesus spoke quite differently. If he quoted ancient authority, he could also quietly set it aside: 'You have heard that it was said to them of old, but I say unto you.' By the manner of his teaching, by his acts of forgiveness, by his promises to those who followed him, he made it clear that he possessed or believed himself to possess true and final authority in the affairs of men. He was asked to state what his authority was or to give some sign to authenticate his claim, but he declined to do so. He placed those who met him in the position where they had to make a decision about *him*. It was not that they could listen to his teaching, weigh it against the standard authorities, and decide for or against its truth; the centre of his teaching was himself, the claim, that is to say, that in him the Kingdom of God had come, that in him the Creator had come to recall his erring creatures to repentance and life, that in him light had come into the world and therefore judgment, full and final judgment. It was upon this claim that men had to make up their minds. And in the end there could only be two possible answers: either the claim was true, in which case the only possible response was the adoration and obedience that men owe to God: or it was false, in which case it could only be punished as the supreme deceit and blasphemy.

In the end, the decision on that issue was clear and for practical purposes unanimous. Jesus was tried, condemned and executed as a deceiver falsely usurping the prerogatives of both God and the King. His disciples were scattered and disillusioned, his body was buried in the earth. Nothing was left of his great claims. And if the story had ended there we may safely say that nothing further would have been heard of them. The name of Jesus would have been forgotten.

The reason why it still haunts men is that God raised him from the dead. By that fact the question which Caiaphas thought he had settled in his court is reopened before a wider tribunal. The question 'Who is this? and what is his authority?' which had formerly troubled the small circle of his contemporaries in Judea and Galilee now faces the whole human race. As before, it is a question about *him*. Is he what the apostolic witness claims him to be?—the sovereign Lord of all mankind, the conqueror of sin and death, the cause and cornerstone of the universe? Or is he deceiver and deceived, still deceiving the world by the false witness of those whom he has deceived into believing the fantastic story of a bodily resurrection? That is the issue. To ask the question, 'Is he

The Presuppositions of Christ's Revelation 59

the one who can save us from disaster, is he the one whose teaching and example can lead us to harmony and peace?', is to show that we have not yet, so to speak, come within range. When you really come within range of the gospel message, even that question becomes trivial. In the face of this tremendous claim, this message from the other side of death, your lips cannot be moved even to frame a question which makes Jesus a mere auxiliary to your own hopes and fears for yourself and the human race. If you want a picture of what it means, so to speak, to come within range of the gospel, you will find it in the words of an early Christian exiled for his faith:

> I turned to see the voice that was speaking to me and, on turning, I saw seven golden lamp stands and in the midst of the lamp stands one like a son of man clothed with a long robe and with a golden girdle around his breast. His head and his hair were white as wool and white as snow, his eyes were like a flame of fire, his feet were like burnished bronze refined as in a furnace, and his voice was like the sound of many waters. In his right hand he held seven stars and from his mouth issued a sharp two-edged sword, and his face was like the sun shining in full strength. When I saw him, I fell at his feet as though dead. But he laid his right hand upon me, saying, 'Fear not, I am the first and the last, the living one. I died and behold, I am alive for evermore, and I have the keys of Death and Hades' (Revelation 1.12-18).

If you are in the presence of one who was dead and is alive and has the keys of death and Hades, the question of authority is answered. And if it seems to you that I have been bemusing you with the experience of men of far-off days, who belong to a different world from ours, let me match that quotation from John of Patmos by a modern story from Russia. In the early 1920's, Bukharin was sent from Moscow to Kiev to address a vast anti-God rally. For one hour he brought to bear all the artillery of argument, abuse and ridicule upon the Christian faith till it seemed as if the whole ancient structure of belief was in ruins. At the end there was a silence. Questions were invited. A man rose and asked leave to speak, a priest of the Orthodox Church. He stood beside Bukharin, faced the people and gave them the ancient, liturgical Easter greeting, 'Christ is risen'. Instantly, the whole vast assembly rose to its feet, and the reply came back like the crash of breakers against the cliff: 'He is risen indeed'. There was no reply; there could not be. When all argument is ended, there remains a fact, the total fact of Jesus Christ, who requires no authority to commend him, but who places every man in the position where an answer has to be given one way or the other to the question that he asks. That fact is the authority for the Christian mission. If we are asked for our credentials, we can only answer: 'In the name of Jesus'.

But what does that imply? If we rest our authority upon the authority of what I have called the total fact of Jesus Christ, we must go on to give our minds to the study of this fact, to ask what it means and what claim it lays upon us. As a starting point for this study, I take the words with which, according to our most ancient records, Jesus opened his public ministry. 'After John was arrested', so the gospel of Mark tells us, 'Jesus came into Galilee, preaching the gospel of God, and saying, "The time is fulfilled and the Kingdom of God is at hand; repent and believe the gospel"'—believe, that is to say, this piece of good news which is now announced. What is the good news? It is that the time is fulfilled and the Kingdom of God is at at hand. The very form of the saying shows us that we are dealing with an event and not with an idea. It is not the promulgation of a timeless truth after the manner of the Indian sages; it is the announcement of an event which brings one era to its close and opens another one, or rather brings it to the threshold. To understand the saying we have therefore to look back and to look forward, to ask what is being fulfilled and how it is being fulfilled. The answer to the first question takes us into the Old Testament background of

The Presuppositions of Christ's Revelation

the coming of Christ; the answer to the second, to the New Testament record and commentary.

We must consider now at least these three elements in the faith which Jesus accepted from Israel, in which his own deeds and words were rooted and without which they cannot be understood. *First* is the faith that the God in whose name Jesus has come is the Creator of all things, the sovereign Lord of time with power to bring one age to an end and to declare the coming of a new one. *Second* is the faith that mankind, created in God's image, is fallen from his true estate and involved in a common sin against the creator. *Third* is the faith that what God is doing in Christ is the culmination of a plan which begins with the choosing of a people to be his own people, to be his witnesses and the agents of his purpose for the world.

1. The Biblical Doctrine of Creation

The fact of Christ must be understood in the context of the biblical understanding of creation. The authority of Christ is the authority of that sovereign will to which we and all things owe our existence.

The importance of this becomes clear when the gospel is preached in a pantheistic or polytheistic context. The Hindu world of today, like the Greek world of the first three centuries, easily and naturally understands Jesus as one of the many divine beings, perhaps the supreme one, to whom men turn in time of need. It is quite possible, in this context, to use towards Jesus all the language of Christian devotion, to worship him as saviour, as lord, as the supreme exemplar of reality and the supreme helper against all the mysterious forces of the universe—against evil, fate, and death. But the centre of the picture remains precisely myself and my need of succour. The biblical revolution which displaces that centre has not occurred.

The context of the Bible is wholly other. Here there is no place for *devas*, for gods to help us against the mysterious and dangerous forces of the universe. There is one God who alone has sovereign authority. Jesus comes with that authority. His coming confronts men with the necessity for a fundamental decision either to accept or to reject him. To accept him means to undergo a radical and total re-orientation of being by which the centre is shifted from the self to him.

But let me here guard against a possible misunderstanding. In saying that Jesus must be understood against the background of the Old Testament faith in God as Creator, I am not asking you to accept another authority alongside of him. I am not, for instance, asking you to accept the authority of the first two chapters of Genesis as something separate from the authority of Christ. Here, as everywhere, the faith is one whole. On what do we ground the Christian faith in God as creator of heaven and earth? On the total fact of Jesus Christ, understood in the true context of that fact, and specifically on the fact of the resurrection. The Old Testament faith in God as Creator, that glorious faith expressed in the repeated refrain 'God saw that it was good', is a faith which looks forward to Christ, looks forward, that is to say, to the day when God will vindicate his sovereignty over the whole world against all the overwhelming evidence to the contrary. The agony with which prophets and psalmists wrestled with the problem 'When will God's righteousness be vindicated in this world?' is an agony which looks forward to and is only fulfilled in the coming of Christ. The Christian faith is that the Day of the Lord dawned in Jesus, and the validation of that faith is in the resurrection of the body of Jesus from the tomb. Here in this created world the rule of God has been vindicated to eyes of faith. It is in the light of that fact that we preach Jesus, not merely as part, even the highest part, of the created world, but also as him through whom all things were made, the cause and cornerstone of the universe.

This affirmation is of great practical importance for the missionary task. The denial of it in various forms of gnosticism is not something merely from the pages of early church

The Presuppositions of Christ's Revelation 63

history but something very much with us today. It is present in Indian attempts to fit Jesus into the pattern of Hindu thinking as one, perhaps the supreme, illustration of the final truth for man, without disrupting the fundamentally pantheistic structure of Hindu thought. It is present in efforts to make the revelation in Christ subordinate to a general category called religion, usually conceived in terms of mysticism. And I think it is present in the controversy concerning demythologizing which recently caused such a stir in Germany and elsewhere. The crucial issue for Professor Bultmann's programme of demythologizing is precisely the resurrection. In his transcription of the traditional articles of the creed in terms of an existentialist philosophy for modern man, cross and resurrection stand together as the inseparable parts of one spiritual experience. But Bultmann ascribes to the cross a historical reality which he denies to the resurrection. He does believe that Jesus died on the cross, but he does not seem to believe that Jesus really rose from the dead in the sense that the tomb was empty on Sunday morning. But surely it is impossible to treat cross and resurrection as a unitary event in the sphere of faith and at the same time to make such a radical dichotomy between them in the sphere of history. This is to put faith and history into two totally separate compartments of the mind. The question inevitably arises, 'What are we dealing with in the sphere of faith? Are we dealing with something which is solely in the realm of inward and spiritual experience, or are we dealing with that which is finally sovereign over the world?' For this question the resurrection of Jesus Christ is crucial. Gogarten in his defence of Bultmann[1] deftly removes both creation and resurrection from any participation in the argument by making at the outset an absolute dichotomy between metaphysics and history. But since the question at issue is the possibility of a revelation of ultimate reality in the sphere of history, this begs the whole question. Modern Hindus think and speak much about the cross. One of the most

[1] F. Gogarten, *Demythologizing and History* (SCM Press, 1955).

common and popular pictures in India today depicts together Jesus on his cross, Buddha under his tree, and Gandhi—three great exemplars of the holy life. It is easy to see that to introduce the idea of the resurrection would shatter the unity which that picture represents. The three figures are together in the picture because the Hindu sees them as three supreme exemplars of his belief that the inward and spiritual is alone truly real. The Christian, in the context of the faith of the Bible, has to ask, 'Where, if anywhere, has this faith been owned and vindicated by the Creator and Sovereign of the world?' and he answers: 'In the resurrection of Jesus from the dead'.

The claim that what meets us in Jesus is the authority of the Creator has great practical importance for the Christian's action in the world. It means that the authority of Jesus is absolute and has right of way over every other claim, and yet does not destroy or override the integrity of the human person. We have been sadly familiar with the fact that a claim to absolute authority by anything in this created world has the effect of destroying the integrity of conscience and reason and thereby enslaving the will. The demand upon us which is made by God in Jesus Christ, while it is absolute and final, does not destroy but safeguards and confirms the integrity and freedom which are his gifts. This is very clear in the record of our Lord's dealings with men. His claim upon them is absolute, having authority over life itself; and yet the response to it must be wholly free. He safeguards the freedom of men to reject him, of disciples to leave him, of Judas to betray him. He meets men with a claim which is absolute but not irresistible, with a truth which is finally authoritative but not coercive. He uses no pressure upon men other than the witness of truth itself, or rather himself. He appeals to no coercive authorities. In the final analysis he offers men himself. Because he is Creator, his claim is for absolute allegiance; but for the same reason in making it, he does not destroy but protects and confirms the rational and moral responsiblity which he has

The Presuppositions of Christ's Revelation

given. That is why those who serve him know that in being his slaves they have found perfect freedom.

This fact has several important implications for the Christian mission. In the first place, it means that in making the gospel known to any race of men anywhere we bring them nothing strange, we bring them the secret of their own being, the revelation of the true source of their own life. We bring them, in effect, the light they already have, the light that enlightens every man. The light we bring may seem strange; it may in fact be strange because of our Christian distortions of it. We have often presented to the world not just the new man in Christ, not just humanity reborn, which is what the Church in principle is, but a variety of national and denominational refractions in none of which the stranger would recognize the true lineaments of the new man in Christ. That is a part of our problem which we shall consider later. What we bring to every man to whom we bring Christ is simply the true light which, if he would but see, enlightens every man. Note that St John does not say the true light that enlightens every religion. It is a recurring and disastrous error to suppose that we are to look for the shining of that light in men's religions. There is nothing in the text to suggest this. It may well be the case that we find the light shining most lucidly in the non-religious elements of pagan culture, in the simple fidelities of home, for instance, and that pagan religion is really in many of its elements, as the Bible repeatedly suggests, a manifestation of the power of darkness; as indeed Christian religion also in many of its aspects may be. The real point of contact between Christian and non-Christian is not in the *religion* of the non-Christian but in his *humanity*. Christ is the light that lightens every *man*. My point is that the Christian missionary is not going out to enrol men under the banner of a tribal deity. We are not inviting strangers to come into our house. We are asking all men to come to their own home where they have as much right as we have. Missions can easily descend into proselytism, into a sort of unconscious cultural im-

C

perialism, if we do not remember this. Christ belongs now as truly to the Hindu and the Muslim as he does to us. He is now their true light. He is not the head of religion, but the head and King of the human race.

A right understanding of the Christian doctrine of creation will help us to a right practice in the matter of *religious liberty*. This is actually or potentially a burning issue wherever the gospel is preached. The claim for liberty is frequently made by missions on wrong grounds. There are, indeed, those who have never really looked at the matter from any point of view but their own, who take for granted the right to preach their doctrines in every situation regardless of the consequences, and to have the protection of the civil power in so doing. We shall not spend time in speaking of this attitude. But on a more serious level there are three views which I think have to be rejected. There is the *Hindu* view which is prepared to allow all religions to co-exist because every religion is seen as merely one possible refraction of the white light of reality. The Christian cannot honestly accept that as the basis for a claim to the right to preach, for it is a plain denial of what he believes. There is the view of *some Roman Catholics*, who apparently claim the right to preach on the ground that the truth has an inherent right to be heard, but who, when Rome is in a position of political power, deny the right to others on the ground that error cannot claim the same rights as truth. It is sufficient to say that this view is incompatible with the kind of authority which we find our Lord claiming for himself. And there is thirdly the view of those who claim *liberty for all views*, even those which appear to be wrong, on the grounds that it is not given to man to have a knowledge of absolute truth and therefore a certain measure of scepticism is necessary in regard to them all. The Christian will certainly agree that he can never absolutize his own understanding of the truth, but he cannot admit that a certain measure of scepticism is in order in regard to the claim of Jesus Christ. He cannot do other then set forth Jesus Christ as the truth. The

The Presuppositions of Christ's Revelation 67

Christian claim for the right to preach the gospel must be grounded on the faith that God has made all men in his own image, that image which is restored to fallen man in Jesus Christ, and that in bringing Christ to men, we are restoring to them their true nature. But it is an intrinsic part of the revelation that it is to be received in freedom because God does not will to destroy the nature that he has created. The Christian must therefore combine a claim for Jesus Christ as the absolute and final truth with a firm protection of the right of men to reject that claim. The acid test of the honesty of the Christian in this regard will be that, when he is in a position of power he will be as scrupulous in upholding the right of the non-Christian to practise and propagate his faith as he is in upholding the right of Christians to propagate theirs.

A right understanding of the Christian doctrine of creation means also that the Christian missionary will have a deep concern to uphold *the proper integrity of the secular order*. One of the errors that has sometimes arisen from the great emphasis in modern Protestant theology on the category of the personal is that the personal has been isolated from the impersonal. It has been forgotten that we only have personal relationships through the medium of impersonal factors, physical, biological, economic, and so forth. The truth is that it would not be possible for human persons to have freedom and responsibility over against their creator if he had not set between them a world operating according to reliable sequences of what, without begging metaphysical questions, we may perhaps call cause and effect. Within this world, diverse human wills have a real though limited freedom to operate and to interact. Without this, there could not be this kind of freedom for fallen human beings. The secular fields of politics, economics, science, and so forth, belong to this created world. They are not ultimately autonomous; they are part of the battleground in which a contest for final sovereignty goes on between God and the devil. But they have a relative autonomy, an autonomy always threatened by demonic powers precisely because God wills to preserve here a sphere for the free decision of faith, which is the only kind of victory he wills to have. Therefore, the Christian who understands the nature of the warfare in which he is engaged will be zealous to safeguard the genuine though provisional autonomy of the secular order as a place wherein believers and unbelievers, men and women of all religions, can co-operate in genuine freedom and equality. This is a matter of great practical importance in the world-wide task of Christian mission to-day. In seeking to safeguard and to be faithful to the conception of a secular state in India, in co-operation in programmes of technical assistance, in the work of Christian colleges and other institutions, the Christian has a responsibility to safeguard the real though provisional autonomy of a secular order wherein men of all religions can co-operate in freedom.

2. *The Biblical Doctrine of Sin*

The fact of Christ must be understood against the background of the biblical doctrine of sin.

According to the teaching of the Old Testament which Jesus accepts and endorses, mankind is a fallen race. The heart of man, made by God and for God, has become the source of all the evil that defiles man. Christ is the light that lightens every man, but when that light came into the world, he was not known. It requires nothing less than a rebirth, the creation of a new nature, to recognize that light. He who would enter the kingdom of God, be he high or low, must be born again, for man, every man, is born into the entail of sin.

Again it is important to say that we are not here setting up the authority of the third chapter of Genesis as a separate authority alongside of Christ. It is Christ who enables us to understand and accept the third chapter of Genesis. It is the total fact of Christ which brings the world under judgment and makes the biblical doctrine of sin not only possible but inevitable. We misunderstand our task, and it is a misunderstanding of which Christian preachers have often been guilty,

The Presuppositions of Christ's Revelation

if we think it is possible to persuade men to recognize their sin *as a precondition* for turning to Christ. It is a rather miserable business, this attempt to persuade the world to accept a pessimistic view of itself in the hope that it will thereby be persuaded to turn to Christ as its saviour. Indeed, it is an impossible proceeding, for how can I take seriously your assertion that you and I and all men are condemned sinners? How can I take seriously a predicament in which I am in such excellent company? The idea that the God of heaven and earth might find the whole human race guilty is one which our human nature, our sinful human nature, cannot conceive precisely because sin blinds us to that possibility. It is the result of our sins that we are all much more concerned about the good opinion of our fellow men than about the judgment of God. It is perhaps a contemporary manifestation of the general fact of sin that we all have in our heart of hearts the good democratic conviction that God will ultimately bow to public opinion.

Nor can we prepare a way for the Gospel by the procedure which Bonhoeffer has described as 'priestly snuffing around in the sins of men to catch them out'. When we say that all men are sinners, we do not mean that if perchance we could, so to speak, get round to the back of even the best of men we would find something base and reprehensible. We are not thinking of the kinds of things we know, perhaps, about ourselves, which we blush to think of others knowing, though certainly these are part of the fact of sin. We are not in fact thinking about the ethical judgment which we men pass upon one another and to which we are on the whole so sensitive. We are thinking of the judgment that God has passed upon us and to which we are insensitive precisely because of the fact of sin. We are thinking of that terrible and glorious event, the one event in human history to which the word crisis is properly applied, namely the cross of Jesus Christ.

Here permit me to return to that popular Indian picture in which the figures of Buddha, Gandhi and Jesus are placed side by side. I have often used that picture as a starting point for trying to explain what it means that Christ brings the world under judgment. For there is hardly any Indian of adult age who cannot vividly remember that terrible Friday upon which Mahatma Gandhi was murdered. They remember and can still feel the moral revulsion that passed through them, through the whole nation, and indeed through the whole world when the facts were known. No man could find words strong enough to express his reprobation of this monstrous deed. If ever there was practical unanimity in the nation and in the world, it was then.

On that other Friday, there was also practical unanimity, but on the opposite side. Men divided upon almost every other issue, religious Pharisees and worldly Sadducees, Herodians and Romans, the governor at one end of the scale and the rabble in the street at the other, all for their varying reasons and from their differing standpoints agreed on this one thing, that Jesus must be destroyed. Even his own disciples concluded that they had been deceived. The practically unanimous judgment of mankind was that he should be crucified. There was no room for Jesus and his claims if human life was to go on. Mankind had seen its maker face to face and with swift and murderous determination had destroyed him.

In that terrible nadir of man's history, there was one silent comment, the suicide of Judas. How shall man live if he is indeed his maker's murderer? And if the risen Lord was to give to men a new possibility of life, what could it be but life from the dead—the life of men condemned, yet forgiven—a life under the words 'I have been crucified with Christ yet I live, yet not I but Christ lives in me', a life under the sign of the cross? No man can stand before the cross of Christ, understanding what happened there and who it was that hung there, and not know that he and all men are thereby brought under judgment, not the kind of moral judgment that we pass upon one another, but judgment in a different dimension, the all-embracing judgment of God, the judgment of him who has

The Presuppositions of Christ's Revelation

judged us by taking our judgment upon himself and bearing with us and for us and as one of us the doom which we have deserved and to which we have been blind. That message breaks upon our human world like the opening up of a new dimension of existence. It is as when you are immersed in all the social life of an ocean liner which has become for the period of the voyage your little world, and then all of a sudden there is an alarm signal: an enemy submarine has been sighted. Suddenly all the questions which filled your mind and all the relationships which constituted your world drop out of sight and there is only question: life or death for you all. It is because we have a message of judgment and mercy for the whole human race, a message from beyond death, that we can and must go to all men, not least to those whose ethical achievement dwarfs our own, and tell them the gospel. Once again, our only authority is what I have called the total fact of Christ. We have a message for the whole human race because in Christ, and in him once for all, the total rebellion of the human race against its maker is unmasked, judged and forgiven.

This has important consequences for the Christian witness to men and women of the higher non-Christian religions. I am thinking here of the simple and searching question which a Christian is bound to ask when he comes in contact with non-Christians who exhibit moral and spiritual qualities that put him to shame—'What right have I to preach the gospel to men better than myself?' Spend a few hours with a man like Vinoba Bhave and ask yourself that question. At the end of such an experience you cannot, I think, fail to feel that here is someone whose moral and spiritual powers dwarf your own; yet he is certainly not a Christian, but teaches doctrines which are incompatible with the central message of the Bible. One cannot help asking the question: 'What right have I to preach the gospel to such a man?'

Here I think we have to recognize that the parable which I used earlier, the parable of the ocean liner, is like most parables, only applicable up to a point. There is no intrinsic relation between the threat of disaster from a submarine and the details of social life on board ship. There *is* a relation between the judgment which is pronounced in the cross upon human nature and the ethical judgments which we pass upon one another. The distinctions which we draw in ordinary life between good men and bad, between pure motives and impure, between higher and lower types of thought and practice, these are not simply blotted out by what happened on the cross. If the words good and bad did not have a real meaning, if they did not describe kinds of character and action which are really different, then the cross would be a meaningless episode; it would not be in any sense a judgment. And yet the cross does, as I have said, open up a new dimension in which our ethical judgments are strangely disturbed. It is the men whom one would ordinarily describe as ethically admirable, the earnest and devout churchmen of the day, who take the lead in destroying Jesus; and those who accept him are the publicans and sinners. The whole situation is summed up in that matchless parable in the final scene of which the elder son, who never transgressed one of his father's commandments, is left out in the cold, and the younger son who has proved a wastrel is inside with feasting and dancing. We are familiar with St Paul's wrestlings with this paradox, both in regard to his own experience as a Pharisee and as a Christian, and also in regard to the deep mystery of the rejection of the gospel by Israel, by the very people who should on every human calculation have been the first to accept it. Israel, who had been entrusted with the revelation of God's will and fought so jealously to keep it, is at the same time the arch enemy of God's will. The gentiles who are 'far off' are found to be near in Christ; the Jews who are near suddenly find themselves far off. Thus does the revelation of the living God upset our human measurement. And yet a deeper understanding such as St. Paul gives us in the long argument of Romans shows us that it is only so that God's mercy can be sovereign over all.

The Presuppositions of Christ's Revelation

I believe that this paradox gives us a clue to the strange fact that it is often the higher religions, and those in them who are ethically farthest advanced, that offer the most bitter resistance to the preaching of the gospel. It is within the terms of this paradox that we can understand our duty and authority to preach the gospel to men better than ourselves. God who created man in his own image has placed in every man and in every race the mark of his origin. There is written deep and in every man's conscience the knowledge that he is not his own, that he is accountable to another and that the claim of that other is one that cannot be weighed against anything else. I do not think that any race of man has yet been found, however primitive, in which there is not some conception of God and some sense of the sacred, however strange may be the objects to which it is attached. And I cannot doubt that here, deep down in man's nature, is the witness to the living God. But—and this is the vital point—that witness alone does not enable man to fulfil God's will. Here we meet the self-contradiction that is the measure of man's sin. Man, estranged from God, has yet the witness to God in his heart. He seeks to build upon that witness the edifice of his religion and his morals. St Paul has shown us once for all how, in the sphere of morals, this effort to obey God's law leads not to union with God but to estrangement. The farther the effort is pressed, the greater the estrangement. The fundamental law is love to God. Man made in God's image is made to love God, to love him with a love which is a free spontaneous response to God's love to him. But man fallen into self-love apprehends God's love as a demand challenging his obedience. The effort to meet that challenge drives him deeper into the mire of self-love because his very effort is centred in a self alienated from the source of love. Love can never be achieved—it can only be received, and then given back. Thus the Pharisee becomes the murderer of Jesus, because the whole edifice of human moral achievement is threatened by the free offer of forgiveness. And thus also the publicans and harlots accept righteousness as a free gift which leaves no room for self-righteousness, and the Pharisee who has spent his life seeking righteousness is left outside.

I am persuaded that this paradox has a much wider application and is the clue to the thing with which we are here dealing. The good non-Christian, who in many cases represents a level of ethical achievement that must make a Christian very humble, is at the same time frequently the bitter opponent of Christian evangelism. Like the Jewish churchmen of our Lord's day, he is both nearer to and farther from the Kingdom of God than the irreligious folk whom we often find flocking into the Church. His religion is certainly not one of mere falsehood or mere illusion. It is the response—in many cases a response which has a nobility and seriousness that puts us to shame—to the real witness that God has placed in the heart of every man. We have no vantage point from which we have any right to judge that response. But the coming of the gospel means quite simply and seriously the end of it. That which all religions seek, namely a true vision of God and a true union with him, can only be the gift of God; and that gift is given in Jesus Christ. Christ is the end of religion in the same sense that he is the end of the law.

This means, incidentally, that in seeking the point of contact for the gospel (and we certainly cannot preach at all unless there is some point of contact) we shall expect to look for it not in men's religion, but in those simple facts of human experience which are—so to say—pre-religious. I mean those elementary matters in which man's consciousness of absolute obligation expresses itself, in the human relationships of home and street and market place. It is an illusion to suppose that it is men's religion which will best enable them to understand the gospel; indeed, if my argument is true, men's religion may be the point at which they are farthest away from any possibility of understanding it. It is significant that the language which our Lord chose to use in giving his message to his contemporaries was—in the main—not the technical language of

The Presuppositions of Christ's Revelation

religion, but the language of ordinary human relationships, above all the language of home.

I conceive, however, that at this point a vigorous objection might be raised. 'Are you being fair?', it may be asked. 'You are practically equating Christianity with God's gift and the other religions with man's effort. Is this fair? Is there not the grace of God in the non-Christian religions? and has there not been plenty of legalism, plenty of human effort and human righteousness in Christianity?' What shall we say to this? Let us take the most outstanding example of a religion of grace outside of Christianity, the faith which is associated with the name of Ramanuja and the philosophical system known as *Visishtadvaita*. Here you have a theology of divine grace in relation to human sin worked out in such a way that it seems almost indistinguishable from the theology of St Paul, apart from the omission of the name of Jesus, and a religious tradition of warm personal devotion to the Giver of grace. May we not believe that God has revealed his grace to Hindu saints in this way, just as he has revealed it to Christians in Jesus? Is the omission of the name of Jesus decisive?

I answer: Yes, it is decisive. It is no part of my purpose to deny reality to the spiritual experience of the Vaishnava saint. I cannot believe that God turns a deaf ear to these outpourings of devotion from men made in his image, or that they arise otherwise than through his witness in their hearts. I cannot believe that there is no contact between the soul and God in these prayers. And yet you have only to get into close contact with a good and godly man of the school of faith we are considering to discover that you are in a totally different world from the world of Christian faith. There is here no solid fact upon which to build your confidence in God's grace. There is, to put it plainly, no revelation of God's grace in action. The only certainly known reality is yourself and your need of salvation. The rest is cloudy and insubstantial. I may be permitted to recall a conversation with a devout Vaishnava who had asked me what I meant by salvation. When I had finished my answer, he said: 'That is exactly what I would have said'. I asked him: 'What, then, is the ground of your assurance that God is ready to forgive you?'. He answered without a moment's hesitation: 'If he wouldn't, I would go to a God who would'. That answer revealed the fact that an apparent agreement covered a totally different understanding of the world. To the man living in the world of the Bible that answer would have been inconceivable. His tongue could not have framed it. For he knows that the one great and awful reality is the God against whom he has sinned. If he does not forgive, there is no other who can. But to the Vaishnava, who could gladly use all the same language as the Christian, the fundamental reality was his own need of salvation; the God or gods who may be asked to provide it are essentially peripheral and insubstantial. There is, I repeat, no revelation of God's grace in action, in events; there is nothing *there* to lay hold on.

I am aware that this last sentence raises immediately another question: can we really believe that the grace of almighty God is really only to be found in a particular series of events selected out of the whole stream of human history? That question falls to be considered in the next section of this lecture. Meanwhile we have to look briefly at the other half of the former question—at legalism in Christianity.

Yes, we must answer very definitely that there has been and still is plenty of legalism in Christianity, and that what I have said about the Gospel in relation to the religions cannot simply be translated into sentences in which 'Christianity' is substituted for 'the Gospel'. More particularly we must confess that the prosecution of the Christian world mission has been and still is shot through with legalism. When we speak of Christianity as the highest of the world's religions; when we set about propagating it as if it were part of our culture; when we confuse evangelism with the business of trying to make other people into replicas of ourselves; when we impose Christ-

The Presuppositions of Christ's Revelation 77

ianity as a law and try to train up 'younger churches' under our supervision to keep it, instead of resting all our practice on the faith that the Holy Spirit can make new men and new communities in his own way; when—in short—we confuse evangelism with proselytism, then we forfeit the right to speak to men like Gandhi and Vinoba Bhave. But that is to forsake our true authority. Our duty and authority to preach the gospel to all men rest upon the fact that God has provided in Jesus Christ one mercy-seat where man's total rebellion is judged and pardoned. Our task is to bring all men to that place. There is no room here for comparing ourselves with others— either to our own advantage or to theirs. Judgment belongs to God. Our business is to bring all men to the one place where the Judge has come to meet us all in order to have mercy upon us all.

3. *The Biblical Doctrine of Election*

The fact of Jesus Christ must be interpreted in relation to the biblical doctrine of election.

Here we meet with an idea which is as offensive to our human reason as it is central to the Bible. The Bible is primarily the story of election, of the people whom God chose, and of the individuals whom he chose to play special parts in the story. According to the Bible, God chose one tribe out of all the tribes of men to be his people, his witnesses, his priests, the agents of his kingship. Again let it be noted that we are not setting up the authority of Genesis and Exodus alongside that of Christ. We understand election, like creation, in the light of Christ's words and deeds. Christ accepted it as his vocation to recall Israel to its true vocation. He reconstituted the chosen people, choosing whom he would and appointing twelve to be the nucleus of a new Israel. These twelve he sent out to be his authorized representatives. Men were to be related to the Kingdom of God by being related to them. To receive them was to receive Christ and to receive Christ was to receive God. Christ is God's chosen and they are chosen in him. To them, and to all who believe, his word is: 'You did not choose me but I chose you'.

This whole conception of election is, as I said, unquestionably offensive to our human reason. How, we are inclined to ask, how can it be that among all the tribes of the ancient world, *one* should be God's people? How can it be that the Christian Church, one particular strand of human history, should be the exclusive bearer of God's saving grace for mankind? The difficulties which this doctrine creates are, I think, of two kinds, metaphysical and ethical. In the first place, it is felt by many people to be self-evident that particular events cannot demonstrate universal truths, that God is present always and everywhere, and that the idea that one particular series of events could be regarded as in any exclusive sense the acts of God, is impossible. In the second place, on ethical grounds it is felt to be unworthy of a benevolent deity that he should show discrimination and pick out one race among others for his special favour. Let us look at these two difficulties.

The first type of objection rests upon assumptions which, if they are taken seriously, ultimately exclude the possibility of belief in a personal God at all. I am not going to attempt even in the most superficial way to consider the whole question of the possibility of this belief. I must simply affirm that there is here a great divide in human thinking, and you have to stand on one side or the other. If it is incredible that a real personal will, however far beyond anything we know of human wills, is at the heart of reality, then we have to accept the consequences of that position. But if we believe in a personal God, we must believe that it possible for him to act and therefore to choose the times and places of his actions.

The second objection rests upon a misunderstanding of the purpose of election in the Bible. It is election not simply to privilege but to responsibility. God's people have constantly forgotten that fact both under the old covenant and under the new and have therefore brought the whole idea of divine

The Presuppositions of Christ's Revelation 79

election into disrepute. But one must answer the objector by putting the counter-question, What is it that you are really asking for? Are you asking for a relationship with God which is in principle accessible to everyone individually apart from any relationship with his neighbour? That is in fact what the unredeemed ego in each of us really wants. At the most secret and central place of our being, do we not constantly want to be in the position where we do not have to be debtor to any other man? We ask: 'Why should I have to go there? Why should I have to do that? Why should I have to depend upon them for the salvation of my soul? Cannot God deal with me directly without bringing another person, another religion, another culture into the business?' The answer is that he can but will not. His purpose is precisely to break open that shell of egotism in which you are imprisoned since Adam first fell and to give you back the new nature which is content to owe the debt of love to all men. And so God deals with us through one another. One is chosen to be the bearer of the message to another, one people to be God's witnesses to all people. Each of us has to hear the gospel from the lips of another or we cannot hear it at all. God's plan for the salvation of the world is a consistent whole, the means congruent with the end. The end is the healing of all things in Christ, and the means therefore involve each of us from the very beginning inescapably in a relationship with our neighbour. Salvation comes to each of us not, so to say, straight down from heaven through the skylight, but through a door that is opened by our neighbour. We cannot be saved except through and with one another, for salvation means making whole. And if it be objected that there is a flaw in that argument because, on this showing, the Jews at least received the gospel through the skylight, the answer is that according to the argument of St Paul in Romans, the Jews also can only be saved in the end through the Gentiles. The salvation of God is a consistent whole. From beginning to end it relates us to God only through a relationship with our neighbour. One is related to God's saving acts not by any kind of direct, unmediated spiritual experience, however it may be formulated. One is related by becoming related to God's people and to the history of God's people, and the central and decisive acts in the history of God's people, which are the substance of the apostolic message.

That statement must at once be safeguarded against misunderstanding. When we speak of the history of God's people, we are speaking of one particular strand in world history, but we are not implying that that is something which exists or can be understood in any kind of disjunction from world history. It is part of world history, that part from which we understand the whole. It is the clue to world history. The Bible, you will remember, does not make any sharp break between the special history with which it is concerned and world history as a whole. The Bible is, so to speak, open at both ends. It begins with the creation of the whole cosmos and with all the tribes of men. Only after this does the story narrow down on the principle of election until it reaches the crisis at which Israel is one Man, and the whole purpose of God for the world is concentrated in the single thread of events enacted on a hill outside Jerusalem. Then at once the story broadens out again. The tribes of men, proleptically present on the day of Pentecost, are gathered in, until at the end we have a vision which includes all the nations and the entire cosmos. The Bible is thus concerned with the whole of human history understood from one centre. And moreover as the story proceeds we are reminded again and again that the special story with which it is concerned is in no kind of isolation from the rest of the world's history but is bound up with it. The God who shapes the destiny of Israel shapes also those of Assyria and Babylon and Tyre and Egypt and Rome; the God who calls Abraham and Jeremiah also raises up Pharaoh and Cyrus. Yet the clue to the meaning of the whole is found in the story of the chosen people. Not that the world exists for the sake of the chosen people; precisely the oppo-

The Presuppositions of Christ's Revelation

site: the chosen people are chosen for the sake of the world. The mission of the Church is the clue to the meaning and end of world history. But the Church does not exist for itself, it exists for the sake of fulfilling God's purpose for the world. It is the people of God in the world and precisely in its concreteness and particularity, it is the bearer of the universal salvation for the world. Therefore we must state, and this is the point that I am trying to make here, that the duty and authority of the Church to preach the gospel to all nations rests upon the fact that God has chosen it for this purpose, to be the witness, the first fruit and the instrument of his saving deeds. He might have chosen others. In the nature of the case, he must choose someone. In the mystery of his will, he has chosen us, the weak and foolish and insignificant. That ought to leave in us no room for pride, but equally it ought to leave no room for disobedience.

One implication of this is so vital that I cannot close without stating it. Everything that the New Testament says about the people of God takes it for granted that it is one people. There is one body as there is one Spirit. Christ has one body, not many, one bride, not a plurality of them. And this one people of God, chosen in Christ before the foundation of the world, the body whose Head is exalted over all things, the ruler of all rule and authority, is not an abstract idea nor a merely eschatological expectation, but a concrete and particular and even sinful body of men and women in Jerusalem and Antioch and Corinth and Ephesus. This is the new man, the new-created human race in Christ, wherein the enmity between Jew and Greek is overcome, wherein men of all kinds and sorts are reconciled in one body through the cross. One has only to call to mind such phrases as these from the New Testament to make it clear that the disunity of the Church is a contradiction of its proper nature and a public abdication of its right to preach the gospel to all nations. We have seen that it is at the heart of the biblical understanding of God's purpose for the salvation of the world, that this purpose is to be effected through a people. This people has its being from God and is the first-fruit and witness and instrument of his saving purpose for all men. The purpose is to reconcile all men to himself in Jesus Christ. But how can those who are not reconciled to one another be the instruments of God's reconciling action? How can he use us to draw all men to himself if we do not let him draw us to one another? How can the world believe our witness to Christ's love if we ourselves have found that love too weak to overcome our natural differences? Our divisions are a public denial of the sufficiency of Christ.

Properly speaking, the Church is just the people of God, just humanity remade in Christ. It should therefore have as much variety as the human race itself. Nothing human should be alien to it save sin. The very vastness of its diversity held together by the single fact of Christ's atonement for the whole human race should be the witness to the sufficiency of that atonement. It should confront man with no sectional or local society, no segregation of people having similar tastes and temperaments and traditions, but simply as the congregation of humanity redeemed, as the family to which every man rightly belongs and from which only sin can sever him. There is, as I have tried to show, an inescapable particularity about the people of God. It is one people chosen out of all the peoples of the earth; that is the scandal of the divine election. But its particularity is in order to be universal. We have by our divisions introduced a wholly wrong kind of particularity, so that men see in it not just the people of God but a variety of particular societies held together, and held apart from other Christians, by some peculiarity of practice or tradition or devotional or doctrinal formulation. Thereby we hide from men's eyes the sufficiency of Christ. Only when we are willing to stake our whole existence as churches on the belief that we have in Christ a unity which can hold us in one fellowship in the truth in spite of the variety amongst us, only then shall we learn for ourselves and show to the world the sufficiency and finality of Christ.

The Presuppositions of Christ's Revelation

It is sometimes objected, perhaps with the tongue in the cheek, that if we had a single Church (a thing of which we do not appear at present to be in much danger) it would have no safeguard against the temptation to absolutize itself; that in fact the divisions of the Church are needed to keep us humble. I cannot agree with this, for two reasons which I will briefly state. First, I do not think it is necessary to believe that history has taught us nothing. The true antidote to the temptation of the Church to absolutize itself is not schism; it is to take seriously the secular order. There you have the true, God-given reminder to the Church that it is still *in via* and cannot treat itself as the absolute vice-regent of God on earth. I do not believe that we shall go back on that insight. And secondly, it is true, though it has not always been true, that our very divisions can help us, help to save us from absolutizing ourselves. Even sin can become a means of grace if it helps to make us humble. Shall we then continue in sin that grace may abound? Doubtless there is no situation in which the Church does not need the grace of God to save it from pride, but I cannot believe that God will ever fail to give his grace to churches which are willing to surrender their separate existence in order that Christ's name may be hallowed and his will for the unity of his people fulfilled.

IV

BY WHAT AUTHORITY?
THE CONTENT OF CHRIST'S REVELATION

WE have been thinking about the words with which our Lord began his ministry: 'The time is fulfilled, the Kingdom of God is at hand, repent and believe the gospel'; and about those fundamental elements in the biblical faith which are presupposed in that announcement: creation, sin, election. I now ask you to look at the announcement itself. It is an announcement of something which has happened and something imminent, of something come and of something coming. This double character runs through the whole development of the ministry of our Lord from this announcement onward. Something has come, but its coming makes us look forward. It is a foretaste, real but not yet complete. The kingdom has come and its powers are at work among us; and yet we pray 'Thy kingdom come'. So it is in the apostolic teaching. The Church is the bride of Christ, yet longs for the marriage feast. We are children of God, yet long for our adoption. We are saved, yet we hope for salvation. Neither the perfect tense nor the future tense can be eliminated. The fundamental meaning of this tension between having and hoping will become clearer as we go on. But let us begin by looking at the two sides of the tension separately, and first at that which has come.

1. *That Which Has Come*

According to his own testimony, the coming of our Lord is the coming into the world of the Kingdom of God. 'If I by the spirit of God cast out devils, then is the Kingdom of God come upon you.' His coming is the inauguration of a new era in human history in which the ancient promises are fulfilled and the Spirit of God is given to man. His claim is quite explicit in the words of his opening manifesto in the synagogue at Nazareth: 'The spirit of the Lord is upon me because he has anointed me to preach good news to the poor, he has sent me to proclaim relief to the captives, and recovering of sight to the blind, to set at liberty those who are oppressed, to proclaim the acceptable year of the Lord.' These new facts, both in word and deed, are the outward sign of a new reality which has dawned upon the world. It is not merely a new teaching, if by that is meant a new formulation of the unchanging facts about the nature of God and man and the world. It is the coming of a new reality, namely the presence of the living God himself among men. The newness of the teaching consists essentially in the fact that it arises from and reports a new reality.

This new reality is not confined to Jesus himself. The same anointing of the Holy Spirit which is given to him at his baptism is given also to his chosen apostles. From the day of Pentecost onward, the same Holy Spirit is at work in them, bringing forth the same fruits. The new reality is let loose into the world in expanding and ever-widening circles as the gospel is carried out from Jerusalem to the ends of the earth. But it is not sufficient to state the matter in this merely external way. We have to try to understand the new reality from the inside. We cannot reproduce the inner spiritual experience of our Lord himself, but we can enter into the inner experience of his apostles and therefore put ourselves in the way of understanding this new reality from within. The clue to the understanding of it is the cross. Between the work of the Spirit in Jesus and his work in the apostles lies Calvary. That free outpouring of the Holy Spirit which was seen in the ministry of Jesus, the incarnate son of God, could only be reproduced in his disciples when they had, in a more than metaphorical sense, been through death and resurrection. They had to go through the experience which St Paul described by saying: 'I have been crucified with Christ, yet I live, yet not I but Christ lives in me.' That experience, as we have seen, is the end of self-righteousness and the beginning of a new kind of being. The dying of the son of God for my sins means the end of any claim of mine to a standing before God. In the face of that fact, I can have no standing ground except what is given to me by his dying for me. The life that was mine is forfeit; the life that I now have is his. The citadel that I kept against him, and over which my flag flew, has surrendered. He is now the rightful Lord. He is free to come in and to take control. What happened at Pentecost, and what has continued to happen ever since, is that the entry of the living spirit of God into the possession of human lives redeemed by Christ is taking place. That possession is seen as a new kind of goodness, the kind of goodness which man knows to be the proper law of his nature but which he cannot produce in obedience to law. It is not a calculated and therefore self-regarding obedience, but an uncalculated and spontaneous overflow of love out of hearts full of the love of God in Jesus Christ.

That overflow into the world is the divine mission to the world of which the Church is the instrument. According to the New Testament, the true witness to Christ in the world is the Holy Spirit himself. When the Counsellor comes, he says 'He will bear witness to me and you also are witnesses.' It is as, and only as they are empowered by the Spirit that the disciples can be his witnesses. Properly speaking, the witness is the Spirit himself. The Church's mission is simply the continued ministry in the world of that same divine Spirit who was in Jesus. His presence in the world means that the new age of the Kingdom has really dawned. The new reality, it must be repeatedly emphasized, is prior to our views about it and is not constituted by our views about it. It is not primarily a matter of our action, though our obedience is involved. The primary mood of it is not the imperative but the indicative. 'When the Holy Spirit has come upon you, you shall receive power and you shall be my witnesses.' Even the great imperative of Matthew 28, 'Go ye into all the world', is undergirded

The Content of Christ's Revelation

by the essential indicative, 'I am with you always to the end of the age'. That is the new reality. We think rightly of the Church's mission to the world only when we base our thinking upon that indicative, a new fact come into the world.

This new reality expresses itself in three characteristic ways: in the existence of a new community based upon a common sharing in the life of the Holy Spirit; in activities which reveal in action the presence of the new reality; in words which bear witness to the new reality.

There is *a new community*. The first fruit of the presence of the Holy Spirit is a community of those who share the new birth, those who have been redeemed through the cross from egocentricity and are thereby placed in a totally new existential relationship with one another. It is not simply the relationship which exists between two people who agree in believing in certain doctrines, or who agree in carrying out a certain programme. Such relationships are important and are included within the relationship which exists between Christians, but they do not constitute it. It is a different kind of relationship involving not a part but the whole of each person concerned. Perhaps the nearest analogy to the total commitment that is involved will be found in the total commitment of a man and a woman to one another in marriage. But even that is only a partial analogy. To understand the relationship involved, we have to go to the central point of the whole Christian experience, namely to the cross. Before the cross, I know that my own life is forfeit. I am part of that human nature that is revealed there as a murderous treason against the Creator. I am condemned there as an enemy of God with no title to exist. But I know in that same moment that I have received a new existence in the fact that Christ died for me. This mighty act of him by whom all things were made is no empty gesture. He, the sovereign Lord of all, has counted it worth while to give his life for mine. He has valued my life as equal to his. He is the Lord and it is his valuation that counts. In the moment therefore of my condemnation I have received a new being which is precisely not my own but his. I live, yet not I—but he lives in me.

But in that situation I never stand alone. My neighbour stands beside me. Christ died for him as for me. Therefore I meet Christ in him. I am put into a relationship with him which I cannot sever without severing my relation to Christ. If I deny him, I deny Christ. He may sin against me, but Christ died for his sin as for mine. If I do not forgive him, I forfeit the forgiveness that I claim for myself. Even if my neighbour is an unbeliever, the fact of Christ places me in this new existential relationship to him. But if he is a believer, if he has accepted for himself what Christ has done for him, then he and I are mutually bound to one another by the same bond which binds each of us to Christ, which bond is our very life. He and I are related to one another as limbs in the same body, as branches in the same vine. It is a relation which concerns the whole of our being and one which cannot be severed without cutting the very sources of life itself. Such is the nature of the unity which properly characterizes the Church. It is not the unity of a sect or party, it is not the unity which arises from an agreed opinion or an agreed programme, it is the unity of a family in which love for one another has become natural, a spontaneous overflow rather than a calculated duty. It is in fact simply the restored unity of the human race created afresh in Jesus Christ. Its inner law is simply the law of all being, which is the love of God. It therefore delivers men both from idolatry and from hypocrisy, and enables them to be simply themselves, to be simply at the service of one another as God created them to be. Within such a unity the natural diversity of race and nation, of temperament and character, of taste and ability, operates to create a richer harmony, reflecting what St Paul calls the manifold wisdom of God (Eph. 3.10). This is the Church as it is set before us in the New Testament, the new human race, the new man in Christ, rooted and grounded in love, learning to comprehend with all the saints the breadth and length and height and depth, being filled with all the ful-

The Content of Christ's Revelation

ness of God, nothing less than humanity redeemed and restored in its true image.

In the presence of such a picture of the Church, we are bound to confess with shame that we have defaced this image almost beyond recognition. We have offered to men an institution, or rather a variety of institutions, each marked by a whole range of peculiarities of structure, thought and practice arising from past history, none of them really capable of being the home of the whole human race. Because the Church is a concrete, visible body it must have a visible structure, but the structure must be such as simply to express the inner reality and make it accessible equally to all men of every race and caste. That given structure includes the scriptures in which every new generation is confronted afresh by God's saving act, the sacraments in which by Christ's appointment we are engrafted and nourished by his living body, and the ministry by which the Church from the days of the apostles onward is preserved in unity of faith and love. Here are the simple but necessary means through which, by the continued working of the Holy Spirit, the new human race is continually related to and nourished by its source in the incarnate work of God. This simple structure leaves room for the widest variety of life and thought. It is sufficient to preserve the unity of the new man in Christ, and it is by returning to this unity centred in the atoning work of Christ that the Church will again be able to manifest before the world the authentic lineaments of the new man, recreated in Christ, the place of which every nation will be able to say: 'This is home.'

The proper mark of this new community will be that *it engages in loving service to the world*. Just as the presence of the Spirit in Jesus meant that healing power flowed from him, so the presence of the same Spirit in the Church will issue in all kinds of loving service to men according to their need. The Church is to be the servant of men. This is not a matter of conscious missionary strategy, though it is part of the Church's total mission. It is simply a matter of being what God created a human being to be. To put it bluntly, if you meet a man in need, and if you are in a position to meet his need, if you are a man in whom the Spirit of God dwells, you will do what the situation requires and there will be no more nonsense about it. The pagan often understands that better than the churchman, as our Lord reminded us in the parable of the Good Samaritan. When the leper comes to him and says: 'Lord, if you will, you can make me clean,' he at once says: 'I will; be clean'. That is not related to any evangelistic strategy. It is the love of God in action. Our Lord took the form of a servant and stooped down to wash men's feet. The Church does not need to apologize when it is found in the same position. She can aspire to no higher title than the one he took: servant. The first outward mark of the presence of the new reality in the world will certainly be e multitude of deeds of loving service to men in their need, whatever those needs may be.

But that will not be the only mark of the presence of the new reality. There will also be *the word*. In our Lord's own ministry, preaching went along with works of healing. In the statement that he made at the very beginning of his ministry, there is the preaching of good news along with the work of healing. Much more must the Church point always beyond its own good deeds to the deeds of God. For the Church, even the New Testament Church, has never been simply an expression of the love of God; it has always been also at the same time a contradiction of the love of God. At no point, therefore, is it sufficient for the Church to point to its own good deeds. It must always be penitently aware of the fact that even the best of its good deeds cannot mediate for man the ultimate judgment and mercy of God. For that there is no place where we can go but to the cross. The Church has therefore to preach Christ afresh to every man of every generation. There is and there can be no substitute for telling the good news. Evangelism, the activity of telling men in words of mouth or pen the story of Jesus, is a necessary and indispensable manifestation of the new reality in action. The word, spoken

The Content of Christ's Revelation

or read, is apt to appear to our eyes a feeble and insignificant thing. Indeed it can often be so; it can fall by the wayside and remain fruitless. But it can also fall into the place where it meets the right response and proves itself to be the mighty power of God, able to transform society, to break open ancient structures of thought and habit, and to bring forth new life on a tremendous scale.

The relation between these two things of which we are speaking, between service and evangelism, has been a matter of considerable discussion and practical difficulty in the story of the Church's mission. In the first place, they cannot be separated. Preaching which is divorced from deeds of love is without power to evoke belief. Deeds of love which are permanently disconnected from witness to Christ evoke belief in the wrong thing. I know that there are occasions when preaching is impossible either because it is forbidden or because it is irrelevant. I know that there are circumstances when explicit evangelism is inexpedient because there does not yet exist a world of thought in which the words of the gospel can be meaningful. In such circumstances, action is all that is possible, but the Christian will not cease to hope and pray for a change in the circumstances and will be eager to seize the first proper moment at which he may say a word for his Lord. What is certainly wrong is a policy which deliberately silences explicit evangelism and tries to put service in its place. For that can only mean that we are offering men our work in place of the works of God, inviting them to trust in the flesh instead of in the Spirit. The best of our service can never take the place of the cross of Jesus Christ.

But if service and evangelism are not to be separated, neither must they be wrongly related. In particular, service must not be subordinated to evangelism. The Christian works of love should be as Christ's were, a spontaneous outflowing of the love of God for men, not a means to something else. What then is the proper relation between them? The answer, I am persuaded, is that they are not to be directly related to one another, but they are both to be related to what I have called the new reality, the presence in the world of the Holy Spirit of Christ in a new community which is the body of Christ. As we have already seen, in Christ's own ministry both the preaching of the good news and the manifold works of mercy are alike treated as the manifestation of the presence of the new age. They provide together the answer to John the Baptist's question: 'Are you he that is to come or must we wait for another?' And similarly in the Acts and Epistles, we find that the varied gifts both of the evangelist and of them that serve are regarded as all gifts of the one Spirit whose presence is the sign of the presence of the new age. The all-inclusive word, corresponding to the new reality of the Spirit's presence is the word *witness*. Within that total reality, both evangelism and service, both word and action have their place. Both of them can be used by the Holy Spirit for the total work of witness to Christ when they belong to and spring out of the life of the new community which the Spirit creates.

One corollary of this, as St Paul reminds us, is that we must not expect that each individual Christian will possess all the gifts required for witness. We are not all prophets, we are not all evangelists, we are not all gifted with powers of healing and teaching. In the fellowship of the body we must learn to rejoice in the gifts which others have and we lack. How rare it is to find Christians really ready to rejoice in the fact that other Christians have gifts quite different from their own! How constantly we do precisely what St Paul laughed at: the nose says to the ear, 'Because you have a different shape from me you do not belong to the body.' In truth it is only the whole body of Christ, all the parts fitly joined togeher and working in the harmony which mutual love creates, only the whole Spirit-filled fellowship, which can truly be the witness showing to the world the manifold wisdom of God.

2. *That Which Is To Come*

Everything Christian derives from its origin in the gospel an

The Content of Christ's Revelation

inescapable tension between having and hoping, between the *now* and the *not yet*. The coming of the Kingdom in our Lord Jesus Christ is both a fulfilment and a promise. The time is *fulfilled*, the Kingdom of God is *at hand*. The Church, therefore, necessarily has this double character. It is a realization of the new age and also at the same time a promise of the new age that is to come. It is an earnest, a real instalment but not yet the whole. It is a foretaste which because it is the genuine article makes us long for the full realization of what we have tasted. One time-honoured way of expressing this is to say that the Church is in motion, that it is a pilgrim people on its way to the promised land. The end to which it moves is the full realization of the reign of God: 'Then comes the end when he delivers the Kingdom to God the Father after destroying every rule and authority ... that God may be all in all' (1 Cor. 15.24). The Church is on the way to that end. Being on the way means not only existing through the centuries but also being sent across the oceans and the continents. The Church is the instrument of the Kingdom because it is the first fruit of the Kingdom, it is therefore from the beginning a body *sent*. It not merely has a mission; it *is* a mission, the continuation of God's mission. 'As thou hast sent me into the world so have I sent them into the world.' Even in the passages which speak about abiding in Christ as branches in the vine, passages which have been often used to support a static conception of the Church, the element of movement, of mission is still present. It is precisely in the context of that parable of the vine that our Lord says to his disciples: 'I chose you and appointed you that you should go and bear fruit.' The whole passage (John 15) makes it clear that the fruit they are to bear is men and women converted to Christ and grafted in the true vine. They can only abide in Christ if they are sent into the world as he was sent. The Church is a dynamic not a static reality, a mission not completed until God's reign is fully established and he is all in all. It exists as the first-fruit and witness and instrument of God's will to sum up all things in Christ.

And yet this fulfilment is not merely future. Jesus who is the end is also the way. The Holy Spirit of God in whom the end is fully known and willed is present here with the Church now. The Church is, according to the New Testament, living now in the last days. There is thus a tension of having and hoping which runs right through the whole life of the Church and through that of every Christian. What Christian is there who does not know something about this tension in his own life? 'Even we who have the first fruits of the Spirit,' says St Paul, 'groan inwardly as we wait for our adoption as sons, the redemption of the body.' We would fain be what God has made us and what nevertheless we are not, children of God. But there is another power in us and in the world, a power not yet subdued, the power of the ruler of this world. We are involved, therefore in a ceaseless warfare. But if this struggle is painful, it is not meaningless. Our groaning, says the apostle, is only part of the travail of the whole creation which waits for the full revelation of the glorious liberty of the children of God. That consummation concerns all men and the whole creation. We have the first fruit of it in the Spirit who is given to us, but we cannot have the full fruition of it till it is complete. The Spirit himself begets in us a living hope for that completion. But it is not a merely passive hope. The Spirit sends us out to be the witnesses of this salvation to the end of the earth so that the consummation may be hastened. Thus the real resolution, so to say, of this tension between having and hoping is the world-wide mission of the Church. That inward groaning, of which we all know something, is to have its outward work in a world mission which witnesses in hope to the fulfilment of God's purpose for the whole creation.

3. *The End of History*

We now turn, therefore, to consider the end towards which the mission is directed. Our thesis here is that the Church has the duty and authority to preach the gospel to the whole world, not only because in it the new reality of God's era is

The Content of Christ's Revelation

present, but also because in it the nature of the end to which human history looks is known, known on the basis of revelation. The Church looks to and bears witness to a real end of history, an end which is in the future and which we do not yet see but to which, according to St Paul, we are nearer than when we first believed.

I know that this whole conception of an end of history is rejected by many, including many distinguished Christian scholars. I have not the time nor the competence to go into all the issues which this question raises, but I will simply say, with what you must forgive as perhaps an extreme naïvety, that it seems to me plain that if history has no end, it has no meaning. The whole idea of a world history, of a philosophy of history, of the history of mankind as a whole, as a meaningful story, has arisen upon the basis of the Christian revelation. One can tell the story of a tribe, of a nation, of a civilization, without raising questions of the beginning and end of history as a whole. But you cannot tell the story without speaking of the beginning and the end of that tribe or that nation or that civilization. There can be no *universal* history, no attempt to construct a meaningful story out of the almost infinite quantity of material concerning the human race, except there be some principle of selection; and there cannot be a principle of selection if there be not some belief about the story as a whole which must include its beginning and its end. But such a belief cannot in the nature of things be a matter of induction from observed events because the essential events are not available for observation, not the beginning and certainly not the end. Of course, if what we call human history is in fact really *process*, process of the kind which can be stated and predicted in terms of the laws of natural science, then induction from observed events is enough. But in that case, the process as a whole is without the element of purpose, and without purpose the whole category of history as distinct from physical science disappears. But if purpose is involved, then induction from currently available phenomena is not enough to establish the character of the whole, for the essential event lies still in the future. The purpose, if there be a purpose, is not yet realized and therefore we can know it only in two ways, either by sitting down and waiting till the end, until we see what happens; or else by allowing the person who has the purpose to tell us. The former possibility is not available to us; the latter means revelation. And in fact, the Western conception of human history as a meaningful story, as distinct, for instance, from the cyclical view characteristic of the Eastern cultures, is ultimately based upon the biblical revelation.

But that revelation is a consistent whole. The Christian confidence that in the end all will be well is inextricably involved in the whole faith concerning God as Creator, who is the eternal Lord of time, able to bring time to an end; concerning sin, and its punishment; concerning Christ, his death and resurrection; concerning the Kingdom of God. What has happened in the West, however, is that this organic unity of belief has disintegrated. The New Testament eschatology is largely rejected even by Christians. But Western man has, with some notable exceptions, found it impossible to give up the fundamental faith in the meaningfulness of history. Unlike the Hindu who, living in a cyclical world, has never been accustomed to look forward, Western man has had to have some kind of eschatology, some sort of answer to the question, in the end, what? That is surely not an unreasonable question. The question 'Where does this road lead to?' is not a merely academic question, and the disrepute of the word, eschatology, is unfortunate.

The difficulty, however, familiar to us all, is that the road appears to end in death. If we have no reliable report from beyond that formidable road block, what shall we do? One great answer has been to look beyond the death of the individual to the progress of the race. The worker dies, but the work goes on. The true immortality, we are told, is not what we take with us but what we leave behind us for our chil-

The Content of Christ's Revelation 97

dren. In place of the biblical idea of the Kingdom of God, we have the idea of a perfect earthly society for our grandchildren. The struggle to create this society becomes the meaning of human history. Thus Kant, writing in 1792, lays it down as a proposition, tenable in the strictest theory, all unbelievers to the contrary, that the human race has always been progressing towards the better and will always continue so to progress. The difficulty about this belief is not merely that it has been so completely contradicted by subsequent events; the difficulty is inherent in the belief itself. For if the meaning of human existence is found in a society which will exist, let us say in the year 2058 (I refrain from using the better-known date, 1984), a society which none of those now living will see, then all the human beings now living have a merely instrumental relationship to the meaning of history. They are instruments, means to an end which they will never see. I need not remind you of the way in which this inescapable logic has worked itself out in the history of the last few decades. The totalitarian movements which have been willing to liquidate thousands of unwanted human beings in the interests of their new social order have only been acting logically upon the faith which is expressed in some of the nineteenth-century hymns which are still to be found in our hymn-books, the faith that the real meaning of history is to be found in the building of a better social order.

Those who have rightly turned from that doctrine in revulsion have, however, too often seized on what appears to be the only alternative faith, namely that the meaning of human life is to be found in the spiritual history of the individual. The destiny of the individual soul becomes the ultimate goal of the whole story; and the whole drama of human history, of politics, of war, of revolution, the whole story of world history, has no meaning and no ending. It is not a drama, it is the only thing which can quite properly be called a non-stop revue, providing the setting for a series of solo items after which each of the players goes off and receives his bouquet privately in the wings. It is interesting that there are still hymn-books which include John Addington Simmons' purely pagan hymn about the future kingdom of man, and which take the magnificent Christian hymn 'For all the Saints' and cut off the last two verses—thus entirely removing the Christian hope and leaving the saints apparently individually asleep in paradise. Thus, the biblical eschatology is completely destroyed. The whole meaning of life is exhausted in the quest of personal immortality. Ego is once more king, dressed out in spiritual garments. That kind of pietism has often been condemned, but it will continue to reappear if the true biblical eschatology is discarded.

Neither of these two positions is tenable for long—neither meaning for world history by destroying the significance of the human person, nor meaning for the individual human person at the cost of destroying the significance of world history. Yet so long as death bounds our horizons there is no escape from that dilemma, for death removes everyone from world history before it has reached its goal. There is therefore literally no possibility of a tolerable answer to the quesiton of the meaning of history apart from a revelation from beyond death. The Christian eschatology transcends this dilemma just because it has its base in the resurrection of Jesus Christ. Christ in whom all things were created is also he in whom all things are to be consummated. If he were not the one, he could not be the other. The message about him is the message about the meaning and end of all things, not merely of each individual soul separately, but of the whole drama of human history and of the world itself.

Needless to say, the whole idea of an end of human history is meaningless unless there is an order of being beyond the order of temporal successiveness in which we live. And the Christian faith is that there is such an order, that time and history exist because of the will of God who is eternal and whose being transcends time—not in the relative and partial sense in which we with our will and memory can transcend time, but

The Content of Christ's Revelation

in the absolute sense that he is the creator of time, and time is but the form of his action. God calls the whole created order into being, sustains it in being, and has power to bring it to its proper end. And the coming of Jesus is the revelation of that end within the created order; in him the Creator who is both the beginning and the end was present among men, and by the operation of the Holy Spirit he is still present in the community of believers.

But the coming of Jesus was at the same time, as we have seen, the exposing of the alienation of the created world from its Creator. Of that alienation, death is the outward sign. The road block of which we spoke is not there by accident. It is there because sin has so corrupted the created world that man cannot of himself find his way to God. There can be no straight road that leads from this world to the Kingdom of God. The same Immanuel Kant, who believed in the law of progress, nevertheless wrote also this haunting phrase, 'From such crooked wood as that of which man is made, nothing wholly straight can be carpentered'. The Bible puts the same truth in more personal terms: 'The wages of sin is death'.

Jesus accepted death. He accepted the total failure of his mission, his rejection by the people of God, and his betrayal by his own disciples. He accepted these things not as blind necessity, not as hostile fate, but as his Father's will. He accepted completely God's judgment and committed everything into God's hands. From a human point of view, both he and his work were utterly buried in failure. But God raised him up to a new and glorious life, a life which was in a sense communicated even then to those who believed in him. To those who were witnesses of it, it was the breaking in of a new order of being, the lifting of a corner of the curtain that divides this created world from the eternal world of God's glory, a foretaste, a first-fruit of the true end of history whose coming Jesus had proclaimed in his ministry. That foretaste made them sure that his was the rule and authority over all things. The word that more than any other expressed their faith is a verse from the Old Testament which is quoted or hinted at twenty-two times in the New Testament: 'The Lord said unto my Lord, sit at my right hand until I make thy enemies a footstool for thy feet'. That verse expressed precisely their understanding of the time they lived in. Jesus, who had humbled himself to the death of the cross, had been vindicated and exalted. He was at the right hand of God. He would soon be revealed as Lord and ruler of all. The good news had to be preached quickly to all men so that all men should have the chance to turn from their trust in the powers of this world and accept the real though hidden authority of Christ.

But meanwhile also they knew there was a battle to be fought. The powers of this world had resisted Jesus and they would continue to do so. They would be organized to oppose his kingdom. Over against the figure of Christ would appear the figure of antichrist. And this name is not a mere synonym for evil in general. It means that the coming of Christ precipitates God's judgment in such a way that the power of evil is concentrated precisely in the form of antichrist, in a form which is precisely the opposite, the rejection, the negation of Christ. It means that once Christ has come, history centres in him. The issues of world history resolve themselves ultimately, or rather penultimately into the single issue: Christ or anti-Christ. A few decades ago, this New Testament teaching aroused only a sort of amusement. Today, we have an uncomfortable feeling that this figure is rather easily recognized, this Big Brother of George Orwell who offers all men security and peace, who claims to be able to produce a total, all-embracing world order complete with concentration camps and gas ovens for the recalcitrant. This figure who seems to offer the possibility of one world order in which there will be salvation for everyone, is no stranger to us today. We can perhaps understand better than our fathers did the repeated warnings of the New Testament that tribulation and conflict must come, that just as the Son of Man could only enter into his triumph by the way of suffering, so the ultimate triumph of

The Content of Christ's Revelation

the Kingdom of God can only come by the way of tribulation. From the point of view of the revelation of the end and meaning of history in Jesus Christ, we can understand that precisely because it is only in Christ that human history can have a meaning, the last and greatest efforts of the powers of this world must be to organize human history as a whole apart from obedience to Christ, that is to say in terms of the reign of anti-Christ.

The Christian is thus prepared for the worst, but he knows that the victory is Christ's. He knows, and here his faith rests upon the resurrection of Jesus from the dead, that though the world lies in the evil one, Jesus has overcome the world, that the end of all things is his reign. Therefore, in every situation, even in the situation which is humanly speaking hopeless, the Christian can act with confidence and with a sense of direction because his direction is—for Christ. His actions do not derive their final significance from the contribution that they make to the history of mankind; they must be directed to making a contribution to the history of mankind, but they derive their final significance from the fact that they are directed to Christ, offered to him for his Kingdom. In Albert Schweitzer's admirable phrase, the Christian's every action will be a prayer for the coming of the Kingdom. The actions do not of themselves create or build the Kingdom; they are, so to say, acted prayers that God will bring his Kingdom, which is his alone. But they are actions in the world, actions which witness to God's reign over the world. For though the world lies in the evil one and though its fashion is to pass away, God's purpose is not to destroy the world but to recreate it, to make new heavens and a new earth. If it be asked what is the relation between this present world and that new one of which we speak, the question can only be answered with such a parable as was used by our Lord and by St Paul himself, the parable of the grain of wheat which falls into the earth and dies and by so doing bears fruit. The Christian can cast his grain into the earth with confidence in the harvest, because he has seen the first fruit in the resurrection of Jesus from the dead. This is not an escapist other-worldliness. It is only this faith which enables the Christian to affirm the goodness of the created world, to affirm human rights, the right of the ordinary man, in the face of apparently overwhelming negations of it. It is this faith, this resurrection faith in a new heaven and a new earth, that could enable for instance Pastor Bodelschwing to return a firm 'Thou shalt not' at the risk of his own life, when Hitler's men came with orders to remove a few hundred useless epileptics to the gas oven. It is this faith that can enable us to continue quietly to do the concrete duties which love of our neighbour requires, even when there appears to be no future at all.

We are living in times very different from those in which the doctrine of human progress was developed. We cannot, for instance, share the merriment with which an eighteenth-century writer on millenarianism greeted the information which he found in an ancient tradition that the anti-Christ would bring with him a crematorium. The generation before us felt, as some still do today, that they had before them what Churchill called the broad uplands. We are rather obsessed with the possibility of an atomic holocaust which would surpass all the language of the apocalypse. A truly biblical eschatology will save us from that obsession. We do live right up against the end of history, but the end of history is not World War III; it is Jesus Christ. He who is the end is he also who meets us every day and invites us to commit each day's duty into his hands. He can keep what we have committed to him against that day. That day is still future. If it were not, we would have to say that history has no meaning. But if it were *merely* future we should know nothing about it. It is present in the sense that he is present, present to our faith through the Holy Spirit. The day when we shall see him as he is is yet to come.

But meanwhile, we are given a plain commission. We are to be Christ's witnesses to all the nations. The meaning of this

The Content of Christ's Revelation 103

present time, this time in which we groan, waiting for our adoption, is that it is the time given for the gospel of the Kingdom to be made known to all men so that they may repent and believe and turn to God. And therefore there is urgency. There is not an infinity of time before us. The decades which believed in the doctrine of human progress naturally tended to interpret Christian missions as a slow and gradual permeation of the world by Christianity. The spread of missions was seen in the light of the general evolutionary idea of development which fitted in well with the fact that missions were being conducted by peoples who at the same time enjoyed cultural and economic predominance and were expanding through the world. But this whole picture is different from what we find in the New Testament. There we find a quite different perspective. There is a great sense of urgency. The end is near. The gospel must be preached to every creature. There must be no tarrying for those who will not hear. The messengers must push on as soon as they can to the ends of the earth. That is the task committed to us. The final issue, the day, the hour, of the destruction of antichrist and the revelation of God's Kingdom is entirely in God's hands.

This sense of urgency has sometimes, however, been construed in a way which rightly repels us. One has heard calculations made as to the number of heathen souls who have passed into eternal damnation during the twenty minutes in which the missionary spoke. And the summons to mission has been presented as an obligation to try to stem this infernal avalanche. That is not the perspective of the New Testament. The fundamental missionary motivation and the ground for the sense of urgency lie in what God has done. God has given himself for the world. All the evil in the world does not cancel the fact that God made the world and God loves it. God saw everything that he had made and behold, it was very good. What a wonderful verse to have at the beginning of our sacred scriptures! That remains the solid foundation underneath all the agony of redemption. God's tender mercies are over all his works. He purposes good for all. The same Lord, said St Paul, is Lord of all and bestows his riches upon all who call upon him. There is no distinction between Jew and Greek—that is to say, between churchman and pagan. The same God is rich in mercy towards all.

But that does not mean an attitude of quietism. It does not mean that we need not trouble, for everything will be all right in the end. No; it means mission, God sending his son and his son sending us. For, says St Paul, everyone who calls upon the name of the Lord shall be saved. But how are they to call upon him in whom they have not believed? how are they to believe in him of whom they have not heard? and how are they to hear without a preacher? and how can they preach unless they have been sent? The logic of God's tender mercy is not inaction but mission, the mission first of the Son and then of those whom he sent. That mission is the reaching out of God's love into the world; the deepest statement of its nature is to be found in the words St Paul uses to describe his own mission: 'The love of Christ constraineth us.'

But love in the end claims all. Therefore, love brings man to judgment. The necessary reverse side of God's love is God's judgment. Therefore, the great text in John 3.16 is followed at once by the word about judgment. 'This is the judgment, that the light has come into the world and men have loved the darkness rather than the light because their works were evil.' In the gospel story, we see the shining of this light bringing all things into the light and compelling men either to acknowledge or to reject the light. We see how Jesus tenderly but inexorably leads men to the point where they must accept him as Lord or absolutely reject him. Tenderly, for he never transgresses that boundary which he himself has set around our creaturely freedom, but stands at the door and knocks like any lowly suppliant; yet inexorably, for there is in the end no neutrality. Every soul must in the end be wholly given to Christ or wholly given to the devil.

But, and here is the point now, the New Testament does not

The Content of Christ's Revelation

only show this as a matter of the personal spiritual history of each individual; it also shows the same pattern in world history as a whole. And the two belong together. Man is a body-soul unity, and his personal history cannot be severed from the history of the world. That whole history, and not merely the individual history of each soul, moves to a real conclusion. The agent of that movement is Christ, and the final issue is Christ or antichrist. There is a real meeting, a real drama in world history, leading to a real conclusion. Our individual lives are not separate solo items each of which is to receive its praise or its blame off-stage afterwards. We are part of the whole, and the end to which Christ teaches us to look is not our own private and personal bliss but the victory of his love over the whole creation. And meanwhile, the task given to us is to be his witnesses. The central clue to world history is the Christian world mission.

V

THE PATTERN OF THE CHRISTIAN MISSION TO THE NATIONS

WE have looked briefly at the situation of Christianity in the midst of our increasingly unified world-culture. We have looked at the basis of the Christian claim to be the faith for mankind. We have now to say something of the outward forms and pattern through which the Church is to make good, in this one world of ours, its claim to have in the Gospel the one faith for mankind.

In an earlier lecture I quoted the statement of Toynbee that, if Christianity is to make good its claim to be the faith for our one world, it must shed its exclusiveness and its Western-ness. I gave reasons for believing that the first is impossible. The second must be unhesitatingly accepted. Christianity cannot be the faith for mankind unless men everywhere are able to recognize it as something which is not provincial but universal, something which belongs to mankind as a whole. I will not say that Christianity ought to be at home everywhere, for that is just what it cannot be. As St Paul tells us, we are a colony of heaven. If we know ourselves truly, we shall know ourselves—wherever we are—to be in a colonial situation. Our task today, however, is to make it clear that the Church is a colony of heaven and not a colony of one of the western peoples. It has too often appeared to be just that. The Churches of Asia and Africa do have, on the whole, a markedly Western look. It has sometimes appeared that they have received, along with the gospel, what is now called a package deal—European hymns and harmoniums to play them on, English prayer books, Gothic architecture, American church elections and

German theology. This is the kind of caricature which it is easy to draw, and to laugh at. Certainly there is truth in it. How could it be otherwise? Missionaries are not disembodied spirits. They went as they were, taking their cultural habits with them. Converts frequently became part of the missionaries' family. Churches grew up around and in mission compounds. Those who were cast out of their own homes found a new home with the missionary and learned to do what he did and love what he loved. Understandably they often reacted against the religion which they had left more violently than those who had never faced a similar crisis. The business of sorting out essentials and non-essentials takes time. It is the work of more than one generation to penetrate behind the forms of a religious culture to its deepest essence and to obtain that sure stance within the Christian faith which enables the new church to discriminate between things which are religiously neutral and things which are incompatible with allegiance to Jesus Christ.

The charge against missions that they have been agents of western cultural imperialism is one that must be examined with care and objectivity. Religion cannot be wholly divorced from culture, however strongly the Christian prophetic note of judgment upon all human culture is sounded. It would be foolish to meet the charge with mere denial. The missionary history of the past two centuries unquestionably contains examples of missions which too uncritically accepted identification with western cultural and political penetration. Sometimes this penetration must be judged to have been for the immediate good of the peoples concerned, delivering them from anarchy, terror and injustice of many kinds. Sometimes it cannot be so justified. Yet there is also much to be said on the other side which is often forgotten. On page after page of the history of Asia, Africa and the Pacific Islands, you will find missionaries laying the foundations for the cultural revivals of the twentieth century, reducing languages to writing, revitalizing stagnant languages, rediscovering the forgotten past of ancient cultures and creating a new pride in them, and protecting the living cultures from destruction. You will find them also in countless cases standing up, often alone, on behalf of peoples unable to stand up for themselves against the slave-trader and the blackbirder, the exploiting of cheap labour by industry, and the over-riding of native interests by colonial governments. These things must be taken into account if a balance sheet is to be drawn. The amount of evidence which would have to be surveyed if a fair judgment were to be made on this issue is so vast that it is very difficult to escape the charge of mere assertion. However, the words of Professor Latourette near the end of his magisterial survey of the evidence can hardly be challenged. 'On many fronts earnest Christians, numbers of them missionaries, fought the mistreatment of other races by their fellow-Occidentals. They sought, not without success, to ease the shock of the impact of Western culture upon non-Western peoples, and to assist the latter to a wholesome adjustment to the impinging culture of the Occident.'

Whatever be the balance that we strike in this attempt to assess the positive and negative elements in the missionary contribution to the impact of the West upon the rest of the world, it remains a simple fact of history that the great period of missionary expansion in the past 200 years coincided to a large extent with the period of the cultural expansion of the Western white races. This is simply a fact, about which neither denials nor denunciations are in order. What is required of us now is to recognize that we are in a new historical situation which calls for radical changes in the structure and pattern of the Church's mission to the nations.

The essential elements in the new situation are as follows:

1. The political domination of the world by the white races has ended. The course of history is no longer determined by decisions made in the Western capitals. Western culture as a whole is no longer accepted by the rest of the world as that

The Pattern of the Christian Mission

which has the right and power to dominate and replace the cultures of Asia and Africa.

2. There is emerging a single world culture which has its characteristic expression in the rapidly growing cities in all parts of the world, and which has as its common substance the science and technology which have been developed in the West, and as its driving power the belief in the possibility of rational planning for total human welfare. This world culture is made possible by the existence of modern means of communication and transport.

3. The Christian Church is now, for the first time, no longer confined to a small part of the earth, but is present—normally as a small minority—in almost all parts of the inhabited world.

It is in terms of these facts that the mission of the Church to the nations must be conceived today. In the briefest terms, it must be conceived as the mission of the whole Church to the whole world, with the implication that the Church, wherever it exists and under whatever conditions it exists, is in principle part of the home base for a mission to the ends of the earth, related in a nexus of mutual dependence and responsibility with every other part of the Church in the fulfilment of that mission to the whole world.

The remainder of this lecture will be an attempt to spell out in some detail the practical implications of this definition of the nature of the Church's mission today.

1. The Missionary Character of the Church

In the first place, it requires a recovery throughout the Church of the understanding of the missionary character of the Church itself. This involves more radical changes than are often realized. It is common knowledge that the modern missionary movement took its rise in a time when the great churches were blind to their missionary obligation. It began as a concern of individuals who were moved, through a new birth of the Spirit, to a conviction concerning the need of every man for Christ. The churches were, in the main, indifferent or hostile. 'Missions' therefore began as societies distinct from the churches. In some places, especially on the European continent, they have remained so. But in the course of these two centuries the estrangement between missions and churches has been largely (though certainly not entirely) healed. Most churches teach their members that they are under obligation to support missions, whether these missions are conducted by the church itself through its own agency, or through an independent society. But the relation between 'Church' and 'Mission' remains a relation between two things generally understood to be distinct. The truth that the Church is called, not merely to 'support missions, but to be itself God's mission to the world, is not yet generally understood.

I do not think that we reflect sufficiently upon the fact that most of the fundamental forms of our churchmanship were laid down during a period in which Christianity was a contracting and not an expanding religion, the period in which, hemmed in by the power of Islam and isolated from the great non-Christian cultures of the East, Christendom almost lost the consciousness of the world which was still waiting to be evangelized. Bishop Lancelot Andrewes, writing at the beginning of the seventeenth century when the evangelization of Asia, Africa and the Americas had scarcely yet been dreamed of among non-Roman Christians, could give thanks 'for the more than marvellous conversion of all the world to the obedience of faith'.[1] Christendom had become a self-contained world; the sense that the Church is a body sent into all the world, a body on the move and existing for the sake of those beyond its own borders, no longer played an effective part in men's thinking. This fact is reflected in the fundamental forms of our church life. The ministry is conceived almost exclusively in pastoral terms as the care of souls already Christian. The congregation is seen as a body existing for the edification and

[1] Andrewes, *Preces Privatae*: Prayers for Friday morning.

The Pattern of the Christian Mission

sanctification of its own members rather than for witness and service to the world outside. Our very systems of doctrine tend to be constructed *vis-à-vis* other Christian systems, rather than *vis-à-vis* the great non-Christian systems of thought. And the normal content of a course in Church history has far more of the mutual disputes of Christians than of the missionary advances of the Church and the encounter of the gospel with the non-Christian cultures which it has successively met and mastered.

Like many other missionaries, I have felt the force of this through the contrast with the situation of the Church in areas of fresh advance. In the diocese of which I was until recently bishop, many of the most spiritually lively congregations had as yet no building of their own. One became accustomed to worshipping, preaching and administering the sacraments in a semi-public place—perhaps under the shade of a tree, or on the verandah of a village house. Always on such occasions there would be a circle of non-Christians standing round, watching and listening. There was always the probability that, on the next visit, some of those now standing in the outer circle would be in the centre as candidates for baptism. Thus one was saved from the tendency to think of the Church as something withdrawn from the world to live its own life for itself, and compelled to see the Church as a thing sent out into the world, an expedition rather than an institution, the visible form of the action of God the Holy Spirit in sending his people out to draw all men to Christ.

There is an increasing sense in the older churches also of this missionary character of the Church, and there are devoted efforts being made to recover forms of congregational life and witness which will manifest it in ordinary practice. This recovery of the truth that the Church is itself God's mission might be called one of the great facts of our time. The growing evidence of the paganization of the old Christendom, and the inter-action between missionary experience on the frontiers and parish experience in the long-established Christian communities, have helped this recovery. Its implications are being explored in theology, in pastoral practice, and in the organization of congregational life. But plainly there is a very long way to go before this recovery extends beyond the few pioneers and becomes part of the thinking of ordinary churchmen.

The extension and deepening of this re-conception of the meaning of churchmanship will require the intimate collaboration of older and younger churches. It is, as has already been said, partly missionary experience which has stimulated this re-thinking in the older churches. But in previous decades, the contact between these older churches and the non-Christian religious cultures has been, inevitably, a rather tenuous affair. It has depended upon reports of missionaries and a very rare visit of a younger churchman to appear alongside of the missionaries on the platform at a missionary meeting. The amazing devotion which countless humble Christian men and women have lavished upon the missionary cause has been sustained by an extraordinarily slight contact with the realities which missionaries were dealing with. Today the situation is different. Contacts between the different parts of the world are multiplied. Tens of thousands of Asians and Africans live for longer or shorter periods in Europe and America. Thousands of business men, technicians, and tourists travel in the areas where formerly the only white men were a few missionaries and civil servants. Moreover systematic efforts are now being made, not without success, to propagate Hinduism, Buddhism and Islam in the West. This multiple meeting of cultures creates a wholly new situation for the Christian mission. Emissaries of the 'Christian' West to Asia and the Islamic world frequently take pains to dissociate themselves from Christianity, and appear as apostles of a purely secular gospel of salvation. Heirs of the Christian tradition of the West, conscious of the fearful sickness of Western civilization, turn to the ancient religions of the East as possible allies in their repudiation of the Western tradition. In all this welter of new experiences the Church has to articulate afresh the offer and summons of Jesus Christ as the Way and Truth and the Life for all men. It cannot do so without the collaboration of churchmen from the different cultures whose meeting creates the present turmoil.

On the one hand the churches of the old Christendom imperatively need the help of Christians who have learned to confess Christ in the midst of the worlds of Hinduism, Buddhism and Islam. These are already experienced in facing issues which are new for Western Christians. This is one of the reasons why younger churchmen can sometimes be the most effective Christian evangelists among students and those who are exposed to the present turmoil of cultural mixture. On the other hand the younger churches will need the help of the older in meeting the problems created by the world-wide spread of the Western secularism. The Churches of Asia and Africa have had less experience than those of the West in meeting the spiritual effects of urbanization with all that accompanies it. They will need at this point help which the older churches can give.

The involvement of the ordinary congregation in the mission of the Church to the whole world is thus required to become much more intimate than it has been in the past. The precious but tenuous links of concern which have hitherto sustained it, the occasional reports of a missionary and the support of his work in prayer and in giving, must now be greatly multiplied and diversified. The members of the congregation who have gone abroad as business men, civil servants, or technicians, and the students or labourers from Asia or Africa or the West Indies who have come to live in the parish, will alike be seen as essential elements in the pattern of the congregation's missionary obedience. The congregation will increasingly learn that missions are more than a good cause to be supported. It will learn that it is itself involved in a missionary task both on its own door-step, and at the ends of the earth. It will learn that in this mission it can do nothing without the partnership of its fellow-members in Christ in other parts of the world. It will come to know them as colleagues upon whom it depends and to whom it must be faithful. And it will learn that its very existence and integrity is absolutely bound up with its faithfulness to this missionary task.

One further corollary of this will be a change in the manner in which the 'promotional' work of missions is conceived. Too often this has been exclusively concerned with the particular work, and the particular missionaries to which the denomination and the congregation is committed. Too often an intimate knowledge of, and concern for, this particular work has gone along with a shocking ignorance of the place of that work within the whole pattern of Christian witness in the area concerned and in the world. The foreign missionary interest, which ought to lift men's eyes to the widest horizons, can too easily become strangely constricted. Missionary education today, without weakening the special and personal links of knowledge, giving and prayer which have been part of the secret of the power of the missionary movement, must set them in a wider context, so that men and women who are accustomed by their daily newspapers to concern themselves with the affairs of all the world, may also be able to know what part the Church is playing in the life of the nations. The developments of secular civilization are compelling ordinary citizens to think in global terms. Christians who stand under the mandate of the Saviour of the World ought not to be less informed or less concerned concerning the cause of the Gospel in all lands than the ordinary citizen is concerning the course of secular events throughout the world.

2. *Older and Younger Churches*

If we are to conceive of the missionary task in the terms we are considering—in terms of the mission of the whole Church to the whole world—we shall have to consider also the administrative implications of this conception in the field of partnership between the older and the younger churches. This

The Pattern of the Christian Mission

is a difficult and complex subject. It is easy to sketch a picture of the mission of the Church as the one mission of the whole Church to the whole world. It is easy to talk about it, easier still to sing about it. The trouble is that it does not correspond with the facts. In the first place the Church is not one. We shall come to that question at the end. But, apart from confessional divisions, we inherit the facts bequeathed to us by the period of missionary advances immediately behind us. We inherit a situation in which the younger churches, even when they have achieved autonomy in a legal and constitutional sense, are still very heavily dependent upon the older churches both spiritually and financially. There is a proper dependence between churches of which I have already spoken—a mutual inter-dependence in which each needs the help of the other. But the facts of history have bequeathed to us a different situation from this. The younger church which has developed out of the missionary work of a church in the West still remains, in most cases, and in spite of a sincere intention on both sides to achieve a genuinely equal partnership, tied in a relation of financial and spiritual dependence upon the parent church, a dependence which makes it very difficult for the younger church to develop that true self-hood which comes—whether to an individual or to a church—from knowing that one depends upon God alone and is responsible to God alone. If partnership is understood simply as partnership between the parent church and the younger church in the missionary task in the area of the latter, it must be said frankly that it will not work. Two such unequal animals cannot be yoked together to make a good working team. It is not merely that they are of such unequal size and strength. It is that, as the result of history, they are so much concerned about their relation to each other. A real and free partnership, a partnership in which spiritual responsibility for the major decisions is really shared by both parties, cannot (I believe) be achieved in this relationship even when there is the best will to achieve it on both sides.

I suggest that three things are required.

First there is required a recognition that partnership means the partnerships of all churches in a mission *to the ends of the earth*. It belongs to the integrity of our confession of Jesus Christ as Lord, that we confess him to the whole world. Something essential is lost if this is lost. Therefore it is not a true partnership if we invite the younger churches to be partners with the older in the missionary task in their own area only. The younger church has an equal right and duty with the older to share in the mission of the Church beyond its own borders. The picture of the mission of the whole Church to the whole world will only correspond with the facts if it is accepted that the church wherever it exists is the home base for a world mission. There will only be true partnership between older and younger churches if the latter are taking their place alongside of the former in *foreign* missionary enterprises. It is therefore of great importance that the churches of Asia are already sending out two hundred missionaries to lands beyond their own borders, and that the East Asia Christian Conference is concerting plans to foster and increase this foreign missionary effort.

Secondly there is required, where it is appropriate, joint action by churches of different nations and cultures in projects of evangelization. This is not a proposal for a 'super mission board' which would pool all the resources of missions and conduct global operations financed out of the common pool. This kind of centralization is sometimes suggested as the administrative corollary of the conception of the mission of the whole Church to the whole world. It would certainly be a mistake. All administrative experience indicates that such vast centralizations of control lead to disadvantages which outweigh any possible advantages. What is needed is that, in the many situations where it is appropriate, Christians of different nations and confessions should work together to meet particular situations or to follow up particular openings for new missionary advance. This is needed first for the simple

The Pattern of the Christian Mission

reason that there are many situations in which a team with the necessary competence can only be secured by going beyond the confines of a single tradition. More fundamentally, it is also needed as a witness to the supra-national character of the Christian mission. It is needed, in other words, so that men may be able to recognize in the missionary operation, not the coming of a particular human cultural or political influence but the mission of him who belongs equally to all races and nations, being the Saviour of all.

Thirdly there is required the development of patterns of work in which the bilateral relations between missions and younger churches are supplemented and corrected by being placed in the wider context of a common planning for the whole mission of the church in a certain area. Here we can learn something from the secular world. It is hard for a relationship between two persons, one of whom is always donor and the other always recipient, to develop into a genuine and free partnership. The same is true in the relations between nations. It has proved possible for the United Nations to provide a context in which help could be given from wealthier nations to poorer without destroying freedom of partnership. The representatives of all concerned nations could sit round the table as equals, all potentially contributors and all potentially recipients of aid, even though some are much wealthier than others. Something comparable is needed in the relations between younger and older churches. The Division of Inter-Church Aid of the World Council of Churches has been able to develop patterns of this kind in respect of its operations. There is no reason why similar patterns should not be developed for the tasks of mission.

Concretely this would involve the creation of opportunities by which, after thorough preparation, the representatives of the churches in a given area, and the representatives of the foreign mission boards concerned in that area, could sit together for ten days to survey and assess their total task of mission in that area. In such a meeting the dialogue between an older and a younger church would be supplemented and enriched by a multilateral conversation. Without this enrichment, the dialogue threatens to become sterile. There are things which need to be said to the younger church which its parent church cannot say; they must be said by others. There are equally things which require to be said to the older church which its daughter cannot say; they must be said by others. Such a conversation should be concerned primarily not with the relations between churches but with the unfinished missionary task. It should be the occasion for a fresh summons to all the parties to a deeper commitment to that task. It should provide the opportunity for a fresh deployment of the available resources not only in the light of the accidents of history but also in the light of the tasks to be done. At the end of it, there should be decisions about policy for the ensuing period, decisions to which all the parties would be spiritually committed.

I have come to believe that some such development is the necessary condition for any significant advance in the Church's world mission today. There are great untapped resources for mission; there are vast unmet opportunities. These cannot at present be matched, because we inherit a pattern of relations between mission boards and younger churches which make it almost impossible for the former to adopt a policy of vigorous advance without threatening the spiritual freedom and integrity of the latter. I do not believe that this spiritual problem can be solved within the existing pattern of one-track relations between a single mission board and a single younger church. I believe that the development of such relationships as I have indicated would provide a context in which they could be a genuine partnership and therefore a real and uninhibited advance.

3. *The Groundwork of Partnership*

But, in the third place, this picture of the church's mission to the world today will require an examination which goes

The Pattern of the Christian Mission

beyond questions of administrative structure to questions concerning the substance of the missionary operation itself. We have to ask 'Why it is that we inherit this legacy of one-track relationships? Why have the younger churches become so dependent upon the older churches from which they were evangelized? Is this relationship of dependence something intrinsic to the nature of missions, or is it an accident of the particular history of missions in the recent centuries?'

If one looks at the evidence of the New Testament it seems clear that the kind of dependence of the younger church upon the older which has been characteristic of the modern period was not a feature of the relationship between the corresponding bodies in the apostolic period. It is admittedly dangerous to build too much on the small evidence which the New Testament gives us; and it is certainly wrong to suppose that all the features of apostolic church order and missionary methods must necessarily be reproduced without change in the very different circumstances of the twentieth century. But it is surely a striking fact that St Paul and his colleagues did not establish any relationship between the church of Antioch and the young churches in Galatia and Achaea comparable to the relationship between a modern mission board in Europe or America and the younger church which has come into existence through its evangelizing work. Whereas modern missions have, as a rule, felt that many decades were needed to train a ministry for the young church, and many more decades before 'autonomy' could be granted to it, St Paul seems to have felt that a few months were sufficient to enable him to leave behind a church fully equipped with the ministry of bishops or elders, deacons, and many others. As for the process by which the mission 'grants autonomy' to the younger church, nothing even remotely resembling it can be detected in the New Testament. The Apostle treats the young churches as responsible bodies from the outset, and teaches them that freedom, responsibility, and the status of an adult, belong properly to the Christian as part of what God gives to him in the Gospel.

When these differences are pointed out it is often replied that whereas St Paul was dealing with men and women who had been trained in the school of Judaism, or in the culture of the Graeco-Roman world, many of the converts of modern missions come from communities which are in such a primitive state that they require a long period of tutelage before they are ready for autonomy. But this is a precarious argument. We have the apostle's own word for it that the Church in Corinth came principally from those who were of little account in the world. Evidently the congregations to which he wrote contained many slaves. Certainly they were very far from moral perfection and were capable of alarming deviations in doctrine. And yet, even when he has to warn and rebuke them, or to expose their false beliefs, he never gives the impression that he is writing to a class of trainees. In spite of his apostolic authority, about which he is quite outspoken, he is writing to those who are ultimately answerable to God. He expects to be able to address them as adults.

I think we have to ask ourselves seriously whether we have not, in the missionary practice of the past one and a half centuries, been misled by the fact that missions mostly came from countries with a more advanced culture and a superior political power to countries which were—at that time—culturally stagnant and politically weak. Have we not been misled by this situation into allowing the missionary task to be seen too much as an operation in which the missionary becomes the tutor and director of the young church, seeking to mould it after the pattern of the older? Have we not been guilty of defining the standards required for leadership, and especially for the work of the ministry, in terms of the cultural situation of the sending church—thus ensuring that the young church could not have spiritual autonomy until it had a sufficient number of members who had mastered the higher levels of Western culture? And have we not, by so doing, placed the young

The Pattern of the Christian Mission

church in a position of dependence which is not part of the true, biblical pattern of church relations, but a carrying over into the sphere of the church of relationships derived from the secular world of culture?

I believe that we have to plead guilty to these charges. Qualifications for leadership in the younger churches have been defined too largely in terms of Western cultural and educational attainments, and it is the missions of the older churches which have set these standards. This is in the sharpest possible contrast to the Pauline method. We read that, after a very brief stay in the cities of Galatia, he ordained for them elders and committed them to the Lord in whom they had believed (Acts 14.23). These elders had assuredly not mastered the law and custom of the Church from which Paul came. They would not have been accepted for leadership in the Church of Jerusalem. But the Apostle seems to have been convinced that they were the men whom God had chosen for the oversight of these new congregations, and that the Holy Spirit would equip them with the gifts which they needed for that office. He vehemently resisted the efforts of later emissaries from Jerusalem to persuade them that it was necessary for them to conform to all the standards of the Jerusalem Church, and roundly declared that to accept such a demand would be to fall from the Spirit into the flesh.

There were, of course, important factors in the situation which were different from those involved in the relation of older to younger churches today. And yet the issue between St Paul and the Judaisers was surely in essence the same as the one we are here considering. The issue is one which arises, and must be settled, at the very beginning of the life of the young church, at the moment when the first group of men and women turns in faith to Christ and asks for baptism. The traditional procedure in the modern missionary movement has been to place such a group from the beginning under the tutelage of a catechist trained, paid, and directed by the mission. When that initial step is taken, the rest follows. The new group begins its life in a condition of dependence, and experience shows that it is exceedingly hard—even after many decades—to make the transition to freedom and autonomy. But it is not necessary to begin that way. In my own experience as a missionary in India I have learned, slowly and with much questioning, that there is another way. When a group of men and women comes to ask for baptism, I have learned now that the first thing to do is to find out who are the men or women whose lives have been touched by the Holy Spirit in such a way as to lead them to this decision. When one patiently questions such a group I have always found that there is somebody, or perhaps two or three people, upon whom God has in some way laid his hand, lifting them out of the accustomed ways and driving them to seek this new path. I have come to believe that one ought to begin by regarding that person, or those persons, as the ones whom God has chosen for leadership in the new group. I do not believe that we do right if we elbow that person aside and put into the position of leadership a man of our own choosing who is the agent of our plans. The Holy Spirit, who has called this group into the fellowship of Jesus Christ, can also provide for it the ministries by which it will be nourished and sanctified in that fellowship.

Once this initial decision is taken, the way is then open for the work of catechists, teachers, and pastors who must help the new group to understand the gospel, the commandments of God, and the ways of the Church. Through a great many ministries they must be knit together into the whole fellowship of the household of God and into the understanding and use of the means of grace. In this sense they become dependent on the whole Body, but only in the sense that every part of the Body is dependent on the whole. And it has been my experience that, when this decision is taken at the outset, the new congregation develops from the beginning a vigorous life if its own and accepts naturally and spontaneously the responsibility for bearing witness to others.

The Pattern of the Christian Mission

If this be true, as I am persuaded that it is, then we can welcome without anxiety the ending of the period in which Christian missions were chiefly an operation conducted by the culturally and politically advanced peoples among those who were relatively backward. If we find ourselves once more in a situation more like that of the first apostles, in which the missionary has no secular power or authority behind him, we can rejoice in the hope that we shall learn again the power of the Holy Spirit himself, through instruments of his choosing to bear his own witness to Jesus as Lord, and to convict the world in respect of sin, of righteousness, and of judgment.

The instruments whom the living Spirit chooses for his ministries may sometimes surprise us. They will not necessarily conform to the cultural standards which have been—in most cases wisely—accepted as necessary in the older churches. They may be, like the first apostles, regarded as unlearned and ignorant men. Their qualification will be that they have been with Jesus. But—and here I speak from experience—if they are those whom the Spirit has chosen and anointed, they will, even if they are men of very little education, develop patterns of service and leadership of which the Good Shepherd will not be ashamed.

In saying these things I hope I shall not be thought to imply that there is no need to help the younger churches to develop a more highly trained leadership. It is, on the contrary, our plain duty to share with our fellow-Christians whatever good treasures we have; and there is much good treasure in the great theological traditions of Western Christendom. The younger churches will be better able to serve Christianly in their own cultural situations by achieving a fuller mastery of the culture of the West. My concern is to insist that the attainment of cultural and educational standards set by the West must not be the precondition for the autonomy of the younger churches. True autonomy is given to the young church with the gospel, and woe to the missionary who does not recognize it. Again one must insist that it is the decision which is taken at the beginning which is fundamental. If the true freedom of the young church, its true standing in the Gospel, is recognized from the beginning, there can follow a sharing of cultural gifts which will not destroy its self-hood, but will enrich it.

4. *One Household*

I have sought to indicate three conditions which must be fulfilled if the Church's mission to the nations is to be reconceived in our day as the mission of the whole Church to the whole world. One indispensable condition remains to be stated. It is that there be some substantial progress in the recovery of the Church's unity.

In the context of these lectures this point hardly needs further argument. Important as are the questions of missionary co-operation which we have been discussing, they yet do not go to the heart of the problem. There is one question which cannot be evaded by the man—whether he be of East or of West—who seeks to bring another human being into the fellowship of Christ's people. It is the question: 'What is the body into which I am inviting this man?' At the present time the answer has to be 'One of the several hundred bodies into which, in the course of the cultural and religious history of the West, the Church of God has been divided'. Each of these bodies represents one strand in the complex cultural and religious tradition of the West. Into the making of each of them there have entered not only elements of truth which are of permanent validity for all men everywhere, but also accidents of opinion and practice which arise from, and are inexplicable apart from, the particular histories of the various European and North American peoples. None of them is spacious enough to be the home for the human race.

Those who would present the claim of Christ to be the one Saviour of the world, in the context of this one world-civilization which is coming into existence, must come to terms with this problem. As they stand, our denominations are the splintered fragments of Western cultural history. No one who is

The Pattern of the Christian Mission

aware of the world he lives in can take seriously the claim that any of them is potentially the home for all mankind. The missionary who goes into the midst of the great re-awakened cultures of Asia and Africa with the claim that he speaks in the Name of the Head of the human race, in the Name of him who is neither of East nor of West but of all mankind, cannot evade the question which will certainly be flung back at him: 'If it is true that Jesus is the Saviour of all men, and that all mankind is to be made one family through him, how is it that you who speak in his name are unable to live as one family? If, as you say, the message which you bring is not merely part of the Western cultural tradition, but is something which transcends all cultures and belongs to man as man, how is it that you have not found in it something sufficiently transcendent, sufficiently fundamental, to enable you—with your relatively minor differences—to find a basis of unity? How can you expect us to recognize in your fellowship our true home, when you have yourselves not yet found in Jesus a foundation for a common life as one family?'

This is a question which demands an answer. We can only evade it by evading contact with the non-Christian world. If we intend to maintain contact with that world—whether in East or in West—we shall be forced again and again to ask 'What is the fellowship into which I am inviting men to come?' The attempt to answer that question honestly will lead to a deep self-questioning and penitence in the life of our churches. We are here at a much deeper level than mere administration and policy. We are concerned with the nature of the Church itself, with the visible form and texture of that fellowship into which God wills to draw all men through Jesus Christ. Here we are in a region where we need above all humility, openness, and obedience. None of us has a full understanding of what the restoration of the Church's unity would mean. It must certainly be costly—for our churches as corporate bodies and for each of us as individuals. But nothing is more central to the missionary task of the Church today than this—that there should be such a recovery of the visible unity of Christians that men of every race and culture may be able to recognize in the Church the authentic lineaments of the household of God, the home in which every man is invited to be reborn as a child of the one Father and a brother of the Son of Man.

INDEX

Abraham, 80
Acts 14:23, p. 121
Adam, 79
Africa, 25, 106 f., 109 f., 125
Allah, 32
America, 9, 12, 110, 112, 119
Andrewes, Lancelot, 110
Antichrist, 28, 100 ff., 105
Antioch, 119
Apostles, 123
Asia, 9, 11 f., 25, 106 f., 109 f., 116, 125
Assyria, 80

Babylon, 80
Bandung Conference, 9
Bhoodan, 33
Bible, 17, 20, 32, 40, 48, 55, 65, 76 ff., 80
Big Brother, 100
Bodelschwing, Pastor, 102
Bonhoeffer, D., 69
Boyle, Dr, 34
Buddha, 32, 64, 69
Buddhism, 42, 112 f.
Bukharin, 59 f.
Bultmann, R., 63

Caiaphas, 58
Calvary, 85
Chandogya Upanishad, 36
Chicago, 31
China, 13
Christendom, 10, 14 ff., 27 f., 110 f., 123
Church, 15, 40 f., 46, 51, 62, 65, 77, 81 ff., 86, 88 ff., 93 ff., 107, 109-26; Orthodox, 60
Church unity, 124 ff.
Churchill, Sir W., 102
Colonialism, 10
Community, A new, 87 *passim*
Corinth, 120

Corinthians I, 15:24, p. 93
Cyrus, 80
Daniel, 52
Devas, 61
Division of Inter-Church Aid, 117
Duff, Alexander, 10 f.

East Asia Christian Conference, 116
Egypt, 80
Ephesians, 3:10, p. 88
Eschatology, 27 f., 96, 98, 102
Europe, 9, 12, 16, 27, 112, 119
Exodus, 77

Faith, 44, 48 ff., 56, 61 ff., 68, 106 f.

Galatia, 121
Gandhi, 64, 69 f., 77
Ganges, 47
General Assembly of the Church of Scotland, 10
Genesis, 62, 68, 77
Ghana, 13
Gibbon, E., 31
Gogarten, F., 63
Gospel, 10, 25, 42, 51, 61, 65 ff., 69, 71, 73 ff., 79, 94, 103, 106, 120, 122 ff.
Gramdan, 32
Greek, 104

Harvard University, 41, 46
Hinduism, 11 f., 38 ff., 43, 112 f.
Hitler, 102
Hocking, W. E., 46-53
Hyder Ali, 25

India, 9 ff., 19, 26, 31, 56, 68, 122
Islam, 42 f., 110, 112 f.
Islamic world, 9, 11, 25, 112
Israel, 77, 80

Index

Japan, 25
Jeremiah, 80
Jerusalem, 80, 85, 121
Jew, 104
Job, 55
John 3:16, p. 104; 15, p. 93
John, St, 44, 49, 59, 65
John the Baptist, 92
Judaisers, 121
Judaism, 120
Judas, 70
Jumna, 47

Kancheepuram, 31
Kant, I., 97, 99
Kingdom of God, 20, 22, 25, 27, 58, 60, 68, 77, 86, 93, 97, 101, 103

Latourette, K. S., 108
Luther, 44

Mark 13, p. 23, 60
Matthew 28, p. 86
Maya, 36 ff.
Millenarianism, 102
Mission, 104 f.
Missionary advance, 116; contribution, 108; education, 114; enterprise, 116; expansion, 108; motivation, 103; movement, 9 f.; obedience, 113; task, 113 f., 116, 118, 120
Missions, agents of imperialism, 107-8; spread of, 103
Myres, J. L., 26

Nazareth, 85
New Testament, 22, 24, 28, 44, 49 f., 52, 81, 86, 94, 96, 100, 103 f., 119
Newton, I., 10

Old Testament, 49, 60, 62, 100
Orwell, G., 100

Pacific Islands, 107

Paul, St., 72 f., 75, 79, 85, 88, 92, 94 f., 101, 104, 106 ff., 119 ff.
Pentecost, 80, 85 f.
Pharaoh, 80
Pythagoras, 34

Radhakrishnan, Sir S., 11, 30-41
Ram, 32
Ramakrishna Paramahamsa, 31, 34 f.
Ramanuja, 75
Reality, 19; A new, 85-92
Religious liberty, 66 f.
Revelation 1:12-18, p. 59
Romans, 79
Rome, 80

Saecula, 21 f.
Samadhi, 40
Sankaracharya, 37
Sannyasi, 21
Sarvodaya system of basic education, 32 ff.
Schweitzer, A., 101
Sheol, 48
Simmons, J. A., 98
Time process, 19 ff., 96
Tippu Sultan, 25
Toynbee, A. J., 41-6, 106
Tyre, 80

United Nations, 117
Vaishnava, 75 f.
Vedanta, 17, 35, 38 f.
Vedantin, 36
Vinoba Bhave, 71, 77
Visishtadvaita, 75
Vivekananda, Swami, 31, 34

West Indies, 113
Wilson, E., 17
World Council of Churches, 117
World Parliament of Religions, 31

Zoroastrianism, 20

www.ingramcontent.com/pod-product-compliance
Lightning Source LLC
Chambersburg PA
CBHW072157160426
43197CB00012B/2423